Weird and Wonderful Nature

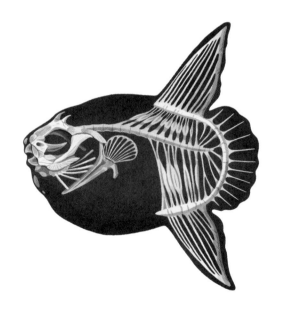

Written by Ben Hoare

Illustrated by Kaley McKean

Contents

Introduction

This book is all about the most unusual natural things on our planet.

It features dozens of bizarre-looking species, all kinds of odd behavior, peculiar weather, remarkable happenings, and mysterious landforms, rocks, and minerals. Many are so unusual you might not believe that they are real—but they certainly are. If you're lucky, you might see some for yourself!

Earth is indeed a weird and wonderful place. And the more we learn about it, the weirder and more wondrous it becomes. Can it be true that there's a spider that can cook? Or that a fungus is able to turn an ant into a zombie? Is there really a sea creature that fires its insides out of its bottom? Or a gigantic bull's-eye in the Sahara Desert visible from space? Amazingly, the answer is yes, and you will discover all these incredible things—and many more—in the pages of this book.

Ben Hoare
Author

Discovering nature

Our knowledge of the natural world has changed a lot over the centuries. Once, there were many legends about mythical plants, animals, and places. Observations and expeditions have since shown us that many of these don't exist, but even now, there is much we don't know.

Myths and legends

In the past, mythical creatures were often thought to be real. Artwork and books showed unicorns, mermaids, phoenixes, dragons, and many other fantastical beasts. Sometimes, these animals mixed imaginary features with those of actual species that people had only glimpsed, or whose remains they had found.

Kappa

Japan is home to the legendary kappa, a river demon with green skin. It is possible that this the monster is based on the Japanese giant salamander, a rare species that can grow to 5 ft (1.5 m) long.

Unicorn

Unicorns appeared in the legends of many European peoples, including the ancient Greeks and Celts. The idea for single-horned horses may have been inspired by whales called narwhals, which have one amazingly long tusk.

Mermaids

Sailors who claimed to have seen mermaids may actually have spotted dugongs. Also known as sea cows, these gentle mammals swim slowy at the surface. They are usually longer than a person and have a dolphinlike tail fin.

Expeditions

Since ancient times, people have launched expeditions to other places to learn more about the world. Before modern transportation, these journeys were frequently dangerous and difficult, but the explorers came back with evidence of all kinds of amazing plants, animals, and other natural wonders.

Humboldt was the first European to describe the strange powers of the electric eel.

Alexander von Humboldt

This German explorer led several expeditions, including a perilous tour of South America in 1799–1804. He mapped rivers and volcanoes, studied Earth's magnetic field, and collected over 60,000 plant specimens.

Merian observed how caterpillars change into moths and butterflies.

Maria Sibylla Merian

Merian worked in the late 1600s and early 1700s, when it was still unusual for women to study the natural world. She went on an expedition to Southeast Asia to study insects in the wild.

Darwin realized the finches on the Galápagos Islands had beaks adapted for eating different foods.

Charles Darwin

Darwin was an English scientist who took part in a famous voyage around the world in 1831–1836. His many discoveries included observations of the unique wildlife of the Galápagos Islands, found to the west of South America.

CHAPTER 1

Species

Nature is full of wondrous living things. We call each different type a species and every one is unique. There are plants with flowers the shape of monkeys, see-through frogs, bearded sharks, jellyfish that age backward, and giant birds with beaks like shoes. But all species, no matter how strange and intriguing, are the way they are for a good reason—their amazing adaptations help them to stay alive.

Zombie ant fungus

This freaky fungus invades the bodies of ants and controls their movements.

Our planet is home to a mind-blowing variety of fungi. These mysterious living things are found almost everywhere. Most feed on the rotting remains of other life-forms, such as dead plants and animals, but the zombie ant fungus is a killer. When one of its spores—dustlike grains similar to seeds—sticks to an ant, chemicals in it dissolve through the ant's tough external skeleton. This allows the fungus to work its way inside, where it spreads and begins to eat the ant alive. Soon, the fungus has consumed so much that it makes up half of the ant's body weight!

Surprisingly, the fungus doesn't infect the ant's brain, but takes control of it by releasing chemicals. The ant soon becomes a zombie, and stumbles around. Then it is made to climb a plant, where it dies, with its jaws locked on a leaf. A few weeks later, the fungus explodes from the lifeless ant to scatter its spores over the ground—and other unsuspecting ants. It's amazing how a fungus, which doesn't have a brain, can take over an animal that does. It's a sneaky, and very clever, way to reproduce.

Stalks of the fungus erupt from the dead ant's head and body.

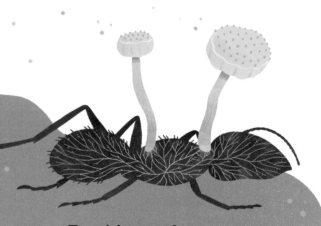

Zombie ant fungus
(Cordyceps)
There are many types of zombie fungus. Most target ants, but others attack caterpillars, wasps, flies, grasshoppers, and spiders. Some even infect other fungi.

Fungus life cycle

First, spores from the fungus land on a passing ant. They burrow inside and feed on the ant's body. Next, they make it crawl up a plant. By making the ant climb high, it means the fungi's spores will spread farther when they are released, starting the process again.

The fruiting cap of the fungus is loaded with spores, ready to fire.

Zombie ants are controlled by the fungus inside them.

Cicada contagion

When a certain type of fungus infects a cicada, the insect's rear end falls off! A white stump grows in its place, which is filled with fungal spores that spread to other cicadas.

In the end, all that's left of the ant is a dry husk.

11

Devil's fingers

When its tentacles open, this stinky fungus resembles a weird kind of starfish.

Fungi have been on Earth for over a billion years. They range in size from microscopic yeasts that are too small to see to giant underground networks of honey fungus that can cover 4 sq miles (10 sq km) and weigh more than a herd of elephants. One of the strangest fungi of all is devil's fingers, also called the octopus stinkhorn. Most of the time, you wouldn't even know it was there because it spends its life quietly feeding on rotting plant material in the earth. But suddenly, in late summer or fall, it emerges above ground. Its fruiting body—the part of it that produces spores—has spectacular pinkish-red tentacles that look like fingers reaching out of the ground. These circle a dark opening that is scarily like a mouth. The fungus also emits an appalling smell. Flies think there is a dead animal nearby, so crawl around the fungus to hunt for rotting meat. They don't find any, of course, but become covered in the fungus's gooey spores. When they buzz off, they take the spores with them, and this is how devil's fingers reaches new places.

Devil's fingers
(*Clathrus archeri*)
Devil's fingers is originally from Australia and New Zealand, but has spread to many other countries, as its spores traveled in shipments of plants, wood, and wool.

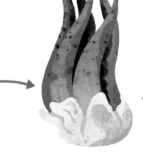

Hatching fungus
When devil's fingers is ready to reproduce, a slimy white "egg" appears. It swells to the size of a golf ball and then uncurls several tentacles. These are smeared with a smelly goo that contains spores. The goo attracts flies, which soon have it all over their legs and carry it away.

Cage fungus

The bright-red fruiting body of the red cage fungus could almost be a piece of sculpture. Like devil's fingers, it smells awful, too.

There are between four and eight tentacles.

The tentacles look like they are made of raw flesh.

The surface of the tentacles is rough and warty.

Sticky spores

A dark, sticky substance like dried blood oozes from the tentacles. Inside it are the spores.

The bell-shaped cap has a woolly texture and soon turns black.

Yellow stagshorn

The fruiting body of this fungus appears on rotting tree stumps and is about the size of your little finger. It might remind you of coral or the antlers of a tiny deer.

The orange branches are soft and waxy.

Shaggy inky cap

At first, this mushroom seems to be a weird egg, but it quickly grows a stalk and cap. The cap darkens and begins dripping black slime, which is thick with spores.

Fungi

Neither plants nor animals, fungi are a separate kind of life. They send out masses of silky threads to collect food, mostly in soil or wood, but all we see are their fruiting bodies. These structures, often called mushrooms, are what release the fungi's seedlike spores. Many fungi are poisonous.

Bird's nest fungus
At first, these mini mushrooms look just like birds' nests full of eggs. However, the "eggs" contain spores, and when splashed with rain, the eggs are flung away.

Collared earthstar
Earthstars burst from the ground like bizarre onions. Their skin soon splits and peels back to make a star, revealing a central dome that is packed with spores.

Scarlet elf cup
If you spot what seems to be discarded satsuma peel, it could actually be this fungus. People used to believe that elves washed in the cups, using them like tiny bathtubs.

Amethyst deceiver
Mushrooms are not just white or brown—they come in all the colors of the rainbow. This purple-colored species is found in forests during the fall, among piles of leaves.

Bleeding tooth fungus
At a glance, the cap of this curious mushroom does look a bit like a big lumpy tooth. There is often red liquid oozing from its surface, as if the "tooth" is bleeding.

Veiled lady
The stem of this tropical fungus is hidden under what appears to be a veil. But, although it is pretty, it reeks like a dead body! The stink attracts flies, which help to spread its spores.

The rainbow plant can be red, yellow, orange, green, or blue.

The plant's leaves are completely submerged.

Growing underwater

Like plants that grow on land, the rainbow plant makes its own food by photosynthesis. It also absorbs nutrients from the river water.

Clear water

The Caño Cristales is famous for the purity of its beautifully clear water. Its fast current sweeps away mud and keeps the water clean, so the rainbow plant is easy to see.

Rainbow plant

When conditions are right, this underwater plant turns the river where it lives into a riot of color.

Hidden among thick forest in the northwest of South America, there is a river like no other—the Caño Cristales. Local people call it the "River of Seven Colors" because of its spectacular change in appearance for just a few weeks each year. The river is shallow and fast-flowing, with many whitewater rapids and waterfalls. Masses of a particular type of river weed cling to the rocky bottom. Most of the time, this plant is not especially colorful and it looks much like any other river weed, but it is resting for now, and waiting for the perfect conditions.

That moment comes when the river's water level, the water temperature, and the amount of sunlight are all just right. During the wet season, between June and December, as the river surges with water from the rains, the river weed suddenly transforms into a spectacular array of colors. Most of its leaves and stems are hot pink, purple, or red, but they can also be a variety of other shades. When viewed with the riverbed, water, and plants, the river looks like a liquid rainbow.

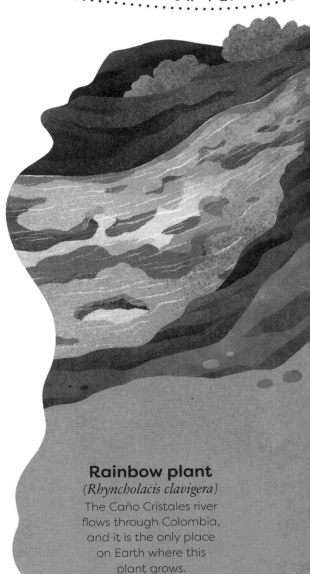

Rainbow plant
(Rhyncholacis clavigera)
The Caño Cristales river flows through Colombia, and it is the only place on Earth where this plant grows.

Rainbow plant
in the sun

Rainbow plant
in the shade

Changing color

The rainbow plant needs plenty of sunlight to develop its full range of brilliant colors. In darker stretches of the river, such as in the shade of rocks or trees, its stems and leaves are bright green.

17

Dragon's blood tree

These rare and peculiar trees bleed when you cut them.

Off the east coast of Africa is a rocky island that's home to many strange plants and animals found nowhere else on Earth. In the dry and dusty mountains of this place, you will come across trees that look like they are upside down! Known as dragon's blood trees, they have unusual root-shaped branches with all the leaves at the top, pointing to the sky. This curious shape allows them to drink from the clouds and fog that roll in from the ocean. Water droplets form on the leaves, then trickle down the branches and trunk to refresh the real roots.

For thousands of years, islanders have cut these trees to harvest a bright red liquid they call emzolo. When it has dried, it is crushed into a powder, which is sold as a red dye. This blood-red fluid may be how the tree got its name, but there is another story. It is said a legendary elephant and dragon fought on the island and after the battle, dragon's blood trees sprang up from the blood-soaked ground.

Leaves only grow at the tips of the branches.

Dragon's blood tree
(*Dracaena cinnabari*)
Dragon's blood trees grow wild on the island of Socotra in the Indian Ocean. Some years, they burst into flower, but the gaps between blooming can be up to 10 years.

Blood-red resin

When a dragon's blood tree is cut, a bright red liquid called resin oozes from the bark. The resin seals the wound, doing a similar job to clotting blood. As the red resin drips from the bark, it looks as if the tree is bleeding.

Rubber from trees

Like dragon's blood trees, the bark of rubber trees is also cut to harvest the fluid it releases. The milky fluid that comes out of rubber trees contains latex, from which rubber is made.

The trees look like huge umbrellas blown inside out.

19

Tilting trees

Cook pines come from the New Caledonia islands in the southwest Pacific Ocean, but have been taken to many other parts of the world. Amazingly, wherever these trees grow, they tend to lean toward the equator! The farther away they are, the more they tilt. No other tree on Earth does this—and no one is yet sure why.

Ghost plant

These spooky plants are completely white and don't have any leaves.

Some forests are home to ghosts. If you head deep into the trees and search in the darkest, dampest places, you might come across them. They are ghost plants, with leafless clusters of flowers so white, they seem to gleam. It's too gloomy here for green plants because they need sunlight to power the process of photosynthesis, which is how they make their food. How do the pale ghost plants survive, then? The answer is that they steal their food instead. They seize sugar and other nutrients from fungi living in the soil. In turn, the fungi take these essentials from trees in the forest. So the plants feed off fungi that feed off trees!

Sneaky organisms that grab what they need from other living things are known as parasites. Thousands of different plants all around the world do it, including the corpse flower, or rafflesia, which has the biggest bloom on the planet. Many of these plant parasites take food from fungi, while the rest get it directly from other plants.

Ghost plant
(Monotropa uniflora)
Ghost plants live in forests in Asia and North and South America. For most of the year, they are hidden underground until they flower in the summer.

Stealing food

Forest soil is full of fungi. They form huge webs made from masses of tiny threads, called hyphae. The hyphae latch onto the roots of trees, suck out sugar, and take it away through their network. Ghost plants steal some of this sugar by sending out roots to connect with the fungi.

Ghost plant roots

Fungus hyphae

Tree roots

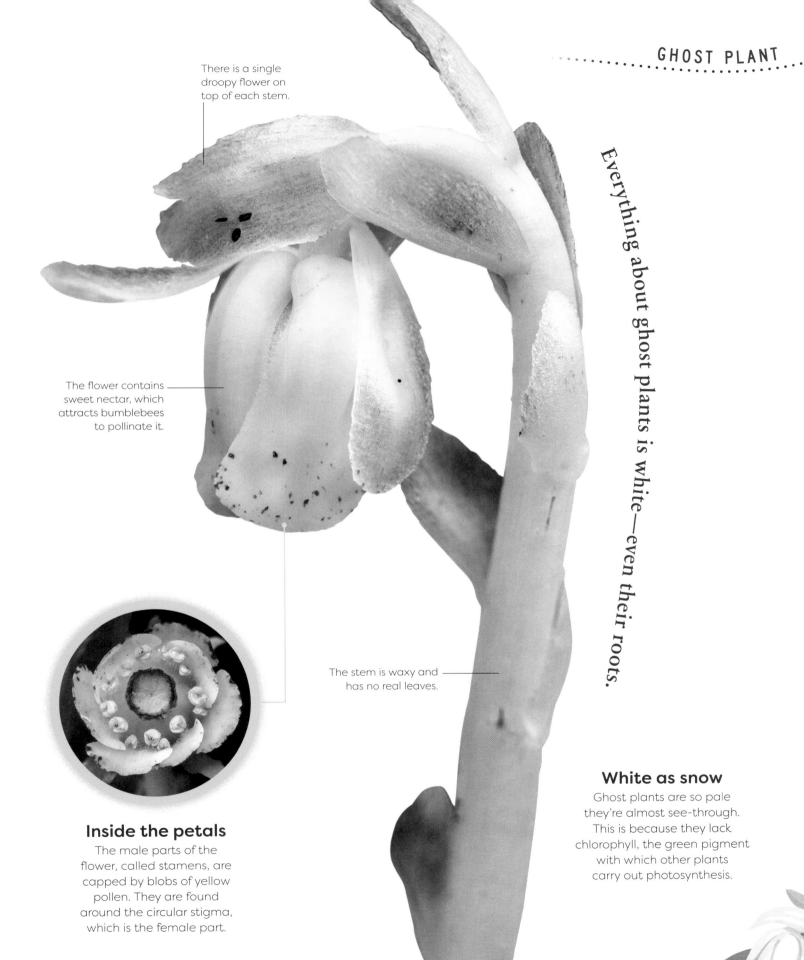

Everything about ghost plants is white—even their roots.

There is a single droopy flower on top of each stem.

The flower contains sweet nectar, which attracts bumblebees to pollinate it.

The stem is waxy and has no real leaves.

Inside the petals

The male parts of the flower, called stamens, are capped by blobs of yellow pollen. They are found around the circular stigma, which is the female part.

White as snow

Ghost plants are so pale they're almost see-through. This is because they lack chlorophyll, the green pigment with which other plants carry out photosynthesis.

23

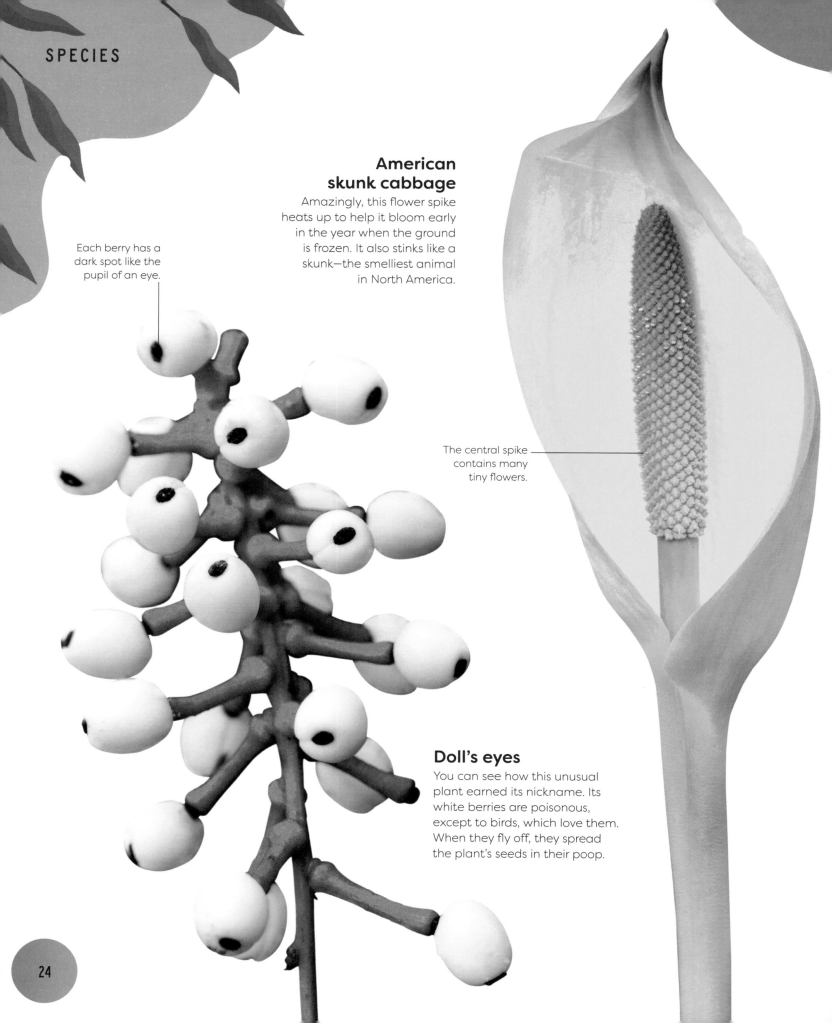

American skunk cabbage

Amazingly, this flower spike heats up to help it bloom early in the year when the ground is frozen. It also stinks like a skunk—the smelliest animal in North America.

Each berry has a dark spot like the pupil of an eye.

The central spike contains many tiny flowers.

Doll's eyes

You can see how this unusual plant earned its nickname. Its white berries are poisonous, except to birds, which love them. When they fly off, they spread the plant's seeds in their poop.

24

Plants

Plants can be every bit as weird and fascinating as animals. Some live as parasites and steal food, some have deadly poison or stings, and a few make their own heat. Many of their flowers do not look like flowers at all—and sometimes smell revolting.

Titan arum

The titan arum has a massive yellow flower spike that can grow as tall as an elephant. The mighty structure gives off an appalling stench to attract pollinators. It lasts only a day before collapsing.

Monkey orchid

Orchids can look like bees, flies, frogs, lizards, and many other animals. This one from South America resembles a monkey, complete with a furry face, two arms, and a long tail.

Flying duck orchid

When a sawfly lands on the lower part of this flower, the "head" and "beak" tilt down to trap it. As the insect tries to escape, it becomes covered in pollen, which it carries to the next orchid it visits.

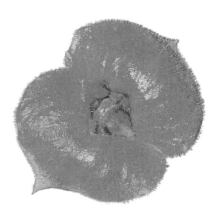

Hot lips plant

This rain-forest plant seems to have a mouth covered in glossy red lipstick. The "lips" are a pair of special leaves that attract hummingbirds to pollinate the small flowers at the center.

Tree nettle

New Zealand is home to this giant cousin of the stinging nettle, which grows taller than a human. Its stinging hairs inflict terrible pain and breathing problems that can kill people.

Vampire plant

This South African plant sucks food from the roots of other plants, so is indeed a vampire. Its bizarre flower reeks of rotting flesh, which attracts beetles to pollinate it.

Fabulous flower

One of the world's oddest blooms, the black bat flower lurks in the rain forests of Southeast Asia. Its huge pair of batlike "wings" are not petals, but a special kind of leaf. Between the wings are more than 20 flowers on stalks and a spray of spectacularly long threads that give this plant another name, "tiger's whiskers."

Feather star

With their spray of "branches" and rootlike legs, feather stars seem more plant than animal.

Often, divers who meet a feather star can't believe their eyes. With a mass of swirling, colorful arms and no obvious head or eyes, the feather star looks like an underwater flower. However, these creatures are related to starfish, and their bodies have the same basic shape, with flexible arms attached to a central disk. They have as many as 200 arms, which are given their feathery appearance by smaller branches, known as pinnules. Like starfish, the arms are covered in thousands of wiggly tube feet that are used to reach out and seize tiny bits of food floating past.

Young feather stars grow up attached to the seabed by a stalk. When they are fully grown, they break free and leave the stalk behind. They get around by crawling or swimming. To swim, they move their arms gently up and down in a kind of slow but beautiful ballet. Many feather stars live in warm ocean waters, but they can also survive in very cold water—there are lots of them in the freezing ocean around Antarctica.

Feather stars
(Crinoidea)
Feather stars can be many colors, including blue, yellow, red, and multicolored. They often live on coral reefs.

If a feather star loses an arm or it is damaged, it can grow a new one!

These unusual creatures look like a fan of feathers.

Filter feeding

A feather star holds up its arms to catch pieces of food drifting past. Tube feet on the arms easily trap the food because they are coated in sticky slime. The tasty morsels are then passed down toward the animal's mouth, which is found at the center of its many arms.

The feather star can hold onto rocks or coral using little "legs" called cirri.

Fixed in place

Sea lilies are similar to feather stars but spend their whole lives fixed to the ocean floor by their stalks. All sea lilies live in deep water.

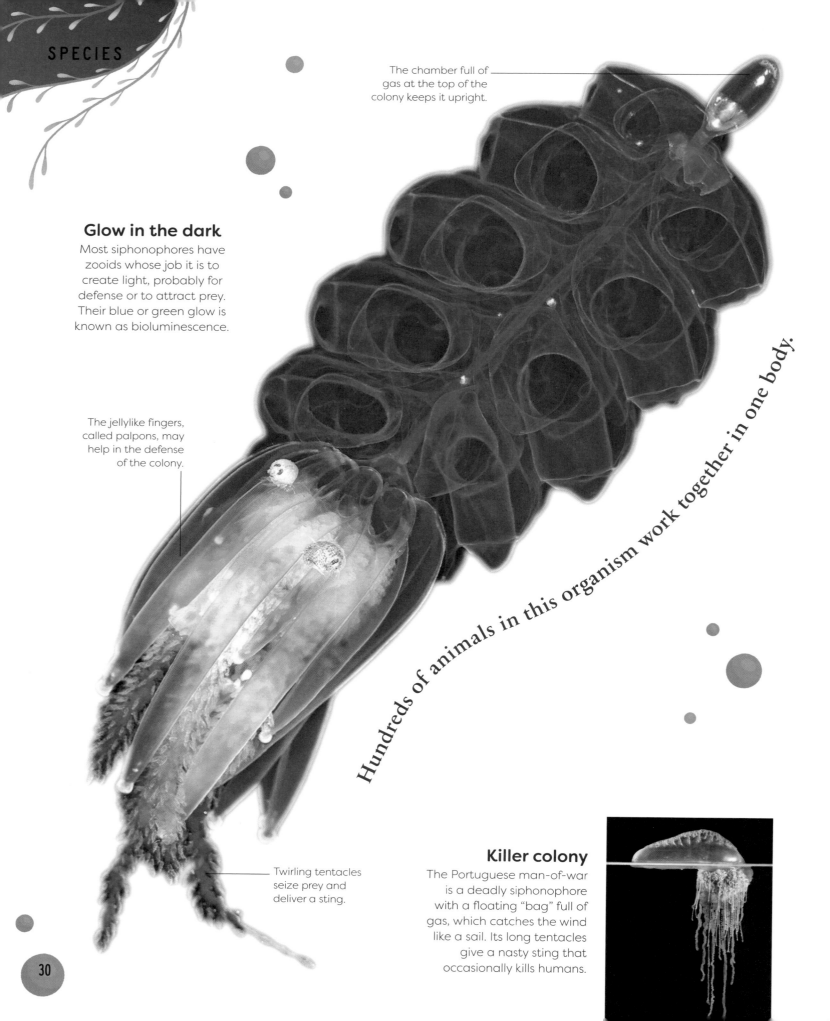

The chamber full of gas at the top of the colony keeps it upright.

Glow in the dark

Most siphonophores have zooids whose job it is to create light, probably for defense or to attract prey. Their blue or green glow is known as bioluminescence.

The jellylike fingers, called palpons, may help in the defense of the colony.

Hundreds of animals in this organism work together in one body.

Twirling tentacles seize prey and deliver a sting.

Killer colony

The Portuguese man-of-war is a deadly siphonophore with a floating "bag" full of gas, which catches the wind like a sail. Its long tentacles give a nasty sting that occasionally kills humans.

Siphonophore

By sticking together, tiny animals can create a much bigger life-form.

Some creatures in the sea are the ultimate team players. They may look and behave like a single organism, but actually consist of a colony of animals sharing the same body and living as one. A siphonophore—pronounced "sigh-fon-oh-for"—lives this way. Its jellylike body has lots of parts, called zooids, each of which is an individual animal. The zooids perform a range of tasks for the good of the body as a whole, just like the organs in a human body. They do this even though siphonophores have no brain to coordinate their actions!

A siphonophore grows when the zooids in it make identical copies of themselves. As the zooids make more and more copies, the colony gets larger. The zooids stay attached forever, until the colony dies or is eaten by a predator. The largest siphonophores live in the deep sea and can be colossal. One giant was filmed and thought to be 150 ft (45 m) long—longer even than the mighty blue whale. However, blue whales are hugely heavy, whereas siphonphores are fragile and boneless, so weigh far less.

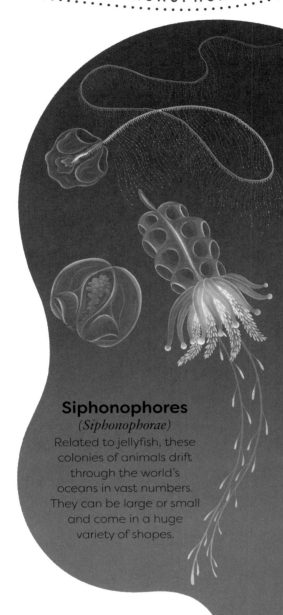

Siphonophores
(*Siphonophorae*)
Related to jellyfish, these colonies of animals drift through the world's oceans in vast numbers. They can be large or small and come in a huge variety of shapes.

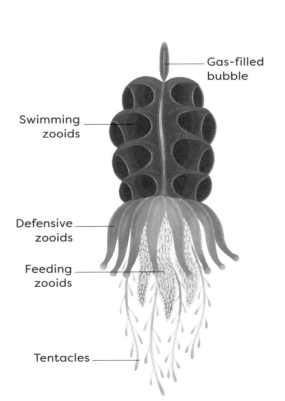

Gas-filled bubble

Swimming zooids

Defensive zooids

Feeding zooids

Tentacles

Different zooids

The zooids in a siphonophore, such as this hula skirt siphonophore, do different jobs. Some of the zooids catch prey with their stinging tentacles, while others help the colony to digest food, jet through the water, produce light, defend itself, and reproduce.

31

Immortal jellyfish

The immortal jellyfish can age backward as well as forward, and live forever.

For thousands of years, people have told stories about humans and animals that never get old and die. Today, we realize these tales are fantasies because living forever is surely impossible. Or is it? The immortal jellyfish really has found a way to cheat death. Like all jellyfish, it has a complex life cycle with many different stages, and spends some time attached to the seabed. Here, it is known as a polyp and looks more like a sea anemone or coral, with arms that wave around to catch tiny pieces of food in the water. Eventually, buds from the polyp detach to become adult jellyfish. However, the immortal jellyfish can also put its life cycle into reverse. If the jellyfish is starving or injured and at risk of death, it stops swimming and shrinks back to a simple blob. The blob drops to the seabed and a few days later grows into a polyp again, which buds off to produce healthy new jellyfish! In theory, the jellyfish can do this over and over, and—if it can keep from being eaten—it may never die.

Venomous sting

Every tentacle is covered in stinging cells. When it feels something move, a cell fires a sharp barb full of venom to paralyze the prey.

Immortal jellyfish
(*Turritopsis dohrnii*)

These little jellyfish are about the size of an eraser on the end of a pencil. They live in seas around the world, mainly in warmer water.

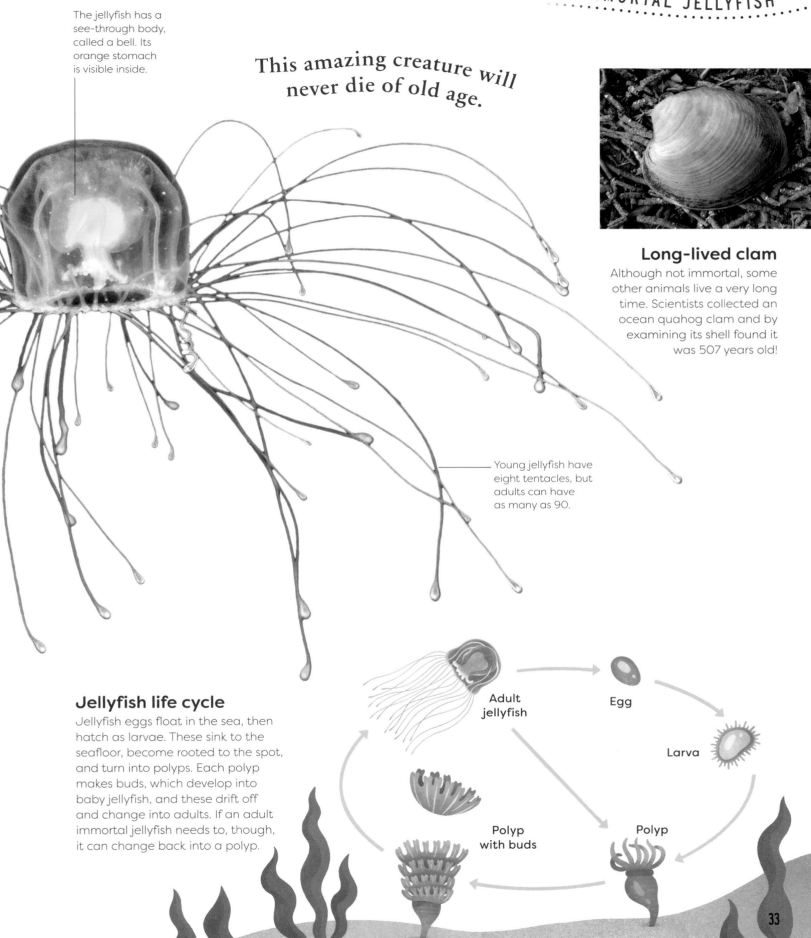

The jellyfish has a see-through body, called a bell. Its orange stomach is visible inside.

This amazing creature will never die of old age.

Long-lived clam

Although not immortal, some other animals live a very long time. Scientists collected an ocean quahog clam and by examining its shell found it was 507 years old!

Young jellyfish have eight tentacles, but adults can have as many as 90.

Jellyfish life cycle

Jellyfish eggs float in the sea, then hatch as larvae. These sink to the seafloor, become rooted to the spot, and turn into polyps. Each polyp makes buds, which develop into baby jellyfish, and these drift off and change into adults. If an adult immortal jellyfish needs to, though, it can change back into a polyp.

Adult jellyfish

Egg

Larva

Polyp

Polyp with buds

33

Sea cucumber

It is hard to tell which end is which on a sea cucumber's sausage-shaped body.

Sea cucumbers aren't really much like cucumbers, except perhaps in shape. Their long, fat bodies are sometimes green, but they can also be covered in colorful patterns. Some even have a shaggy appearance like a textured cushion or knobbly knitted sweater. They seem to slide around the seabed, but actually move on thin legs so tiny they can be difficult to see. Their diet includes any small pieces of food they find, including algae, chunks of coral, and the remains of dead animals.

Sea cucumbers are cousins of sea urchins, starfish, and feather stars, but unlike them, they have no body armor or spines. They are far from defenseless, however, because their flesh is toxic. To scare predators, they can also push their guts out of their bodies! Sometimes, they eject bits of other organs, too. Amazingly, in just a few weeks, their damaged insides will have regrown. So, while firing your organs through your mouth or bottom at an enemy may sound painful, it does sea cucumbers no lasting harm. Some of them make this defense even nastier by filling the disgusting shower of insides with poison.

Sneaky fish

The pearlfish swims up the bottom of a sea cucumber and lives happily inside. Some eat the sea cucumber's reproductive organs—not a pleasant experience for their host!

The leopard sea cucumber has a pattern of orange spots that look like eyes.

Sea cucumbers breathe through their bottoms!

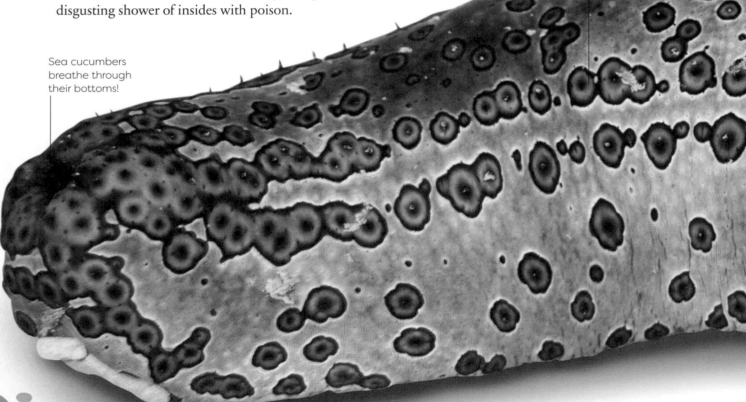

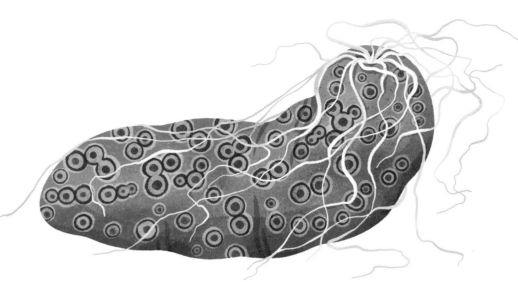

Insides out

When it feels threatened, the leopard sea cucumber squeezes hard with its muscles to fire out a mass of what look like noodles from its bottom. These threads are sticky, and a predator can quickly become tangled up in them, allowing the sea cucumber to escape.

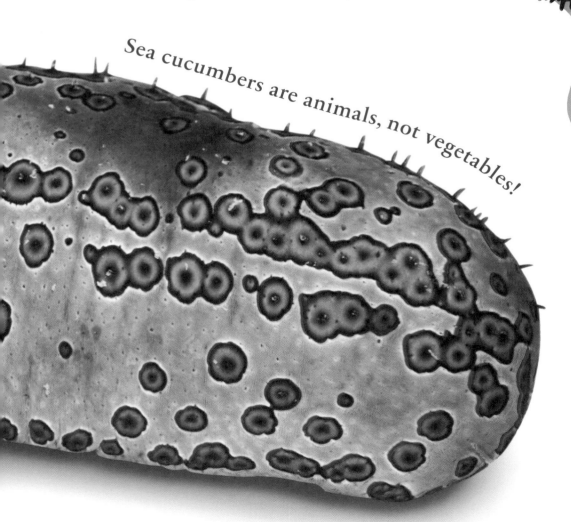

Sea cucumbers are animals, not vegetables!

Sea cucumbers
(*Holothuroidea*)

Sea cucumbers live throughout the world's seas, from sunlit coral reefs to the dark, chilly depths of the ocean. They can be found on the ocean floor in great herds.

Walking cucumber

Hidden on the underside of a sea cucumber are five double rows of tentacle-like tube feet. The sea cucumber uses these to walk slowly along the seafloor.

Swimming snail

Mysterious sea butterflies flutter through the ocean.
They are not insects, which can't survive in salt water,
but a kind of sea snail. Their muscular foot has split
to become a pair of wings that flap to push them
forward. Below these is their spiral shell, which is
see-through, as if carved from crystal.

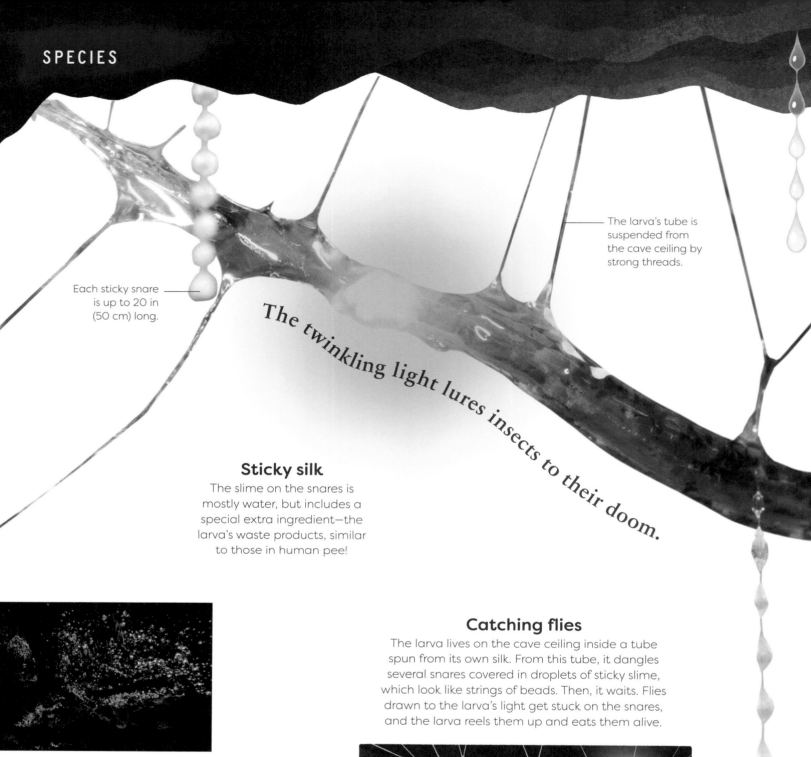

The larva's tube is suspended from the cave ceiling by strong threads.

Each sticky snare is up to 20 in (50 cm) long.

The twinkling light lures insects to their doom.

Sticky silk

The slime on the snares is mostly water, but includes a special extra ingredient—the larva's waste products, similar to those in human pee!

Catching flies

The larva lives on the cave ceiling inside a tube spun from its own silk. From this tube, it dangles several snares covered in droplets of sticky slime, which look like strings of beads. Then, it waits. Flies drawn to the larva's light get stuck on the snares, and the larva reels them up and eats them alive.

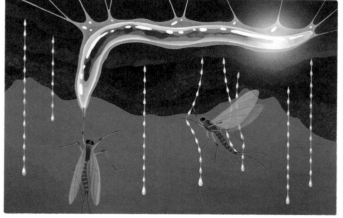

Glowing caves

The Waitomo and Waipu caves are the best-known "glowworm caves." They form part of a huge cave network in an area of limestone rock on New Zealand's North Island.

Fungus gnat

The larvae of these insects glow in the dark, and although they look beautiful, they are deadly.

Deep inside a cave, you would expect it to be totally dark, but this is not always the case. In some caves, bright lights twinkle all over the damp ceiling like a galaxy of stars. The bluish glow is produced by the larvae of a particular species of fungus gnat, which are a type of fly. Because the larvae look a bit like worms, people often call them "glowworms." The glow is not merely for show, but a sneaky way to get a meal. Other small flies living in the cave are attracted by the lights on the ceiling and end up stuck on slimy traps prepared by the waiting larvae. It's like a strange kind of fishing!

The spooky glow made by the fungus gnat larvae is called bioluminescence. Many other life-forms are able to glow, too, from jellyfish and sharks to fungi and fireflies, for many different reasons. The way they do it varies according to the species, but it usually involves chemicals called luciferins. When luciferins mix with oxygen, there is a chemical reaction that gives off light.

Silk for the snares is produced by glands in the larva's mouth.

Fungus gnat
(Arachnocampa luminosa)
This insect is found only in New Zealand, mainly in wet caves, but also in forests where it rains a lot. Similar fungus gnats live in Australia.

39

Glowing life

A dazzling variety of living things glow in the dark. Most make light through a chemical reaction—we call this "bioluminescence." Others seem to change color after absorbing some of the sun's rays or when viewed under an ultraviolet (UV) light—this is "biofluorescence."

Eyelight fish
These small fish have a colony of glowing bacteria living under each eye. The fish are able to quickly cover and uncover this area with a flap of skin, so that the light appears to flash on and off.

Comb jelly
The oceans are full of these jellylike animals, many of which glow. Some also appear to shimmer with rainbow colors, but this is different from glowing—these colors are made when light reflects off rows of tiny hairs.

Northern flying squirrel
Several kinds of mammal have unusual fur that is fluorescent under UV light. For example, North America's flying squirrels glow pink, while Australia's wombat and duck-billed platypus have a blue-green shine.

Lantern shark
These deep-sea dwellers have light-producing organs on their undersides and fins. This helps them blend in with the faint glimmer of light coming from above, hiding them from predators.

Tiger salamander
The yellow skin on these salamanders looks bright green to us when a UV light is shone on it. Many other amphibians are biofluorescent, too, but scientists aren't sure why.

Bitter oyster fungus
These fungi contain a chemical which gives them a bizarre green glow during the night. It's possible that the fungi may glow to attract insects that will spread their spores.

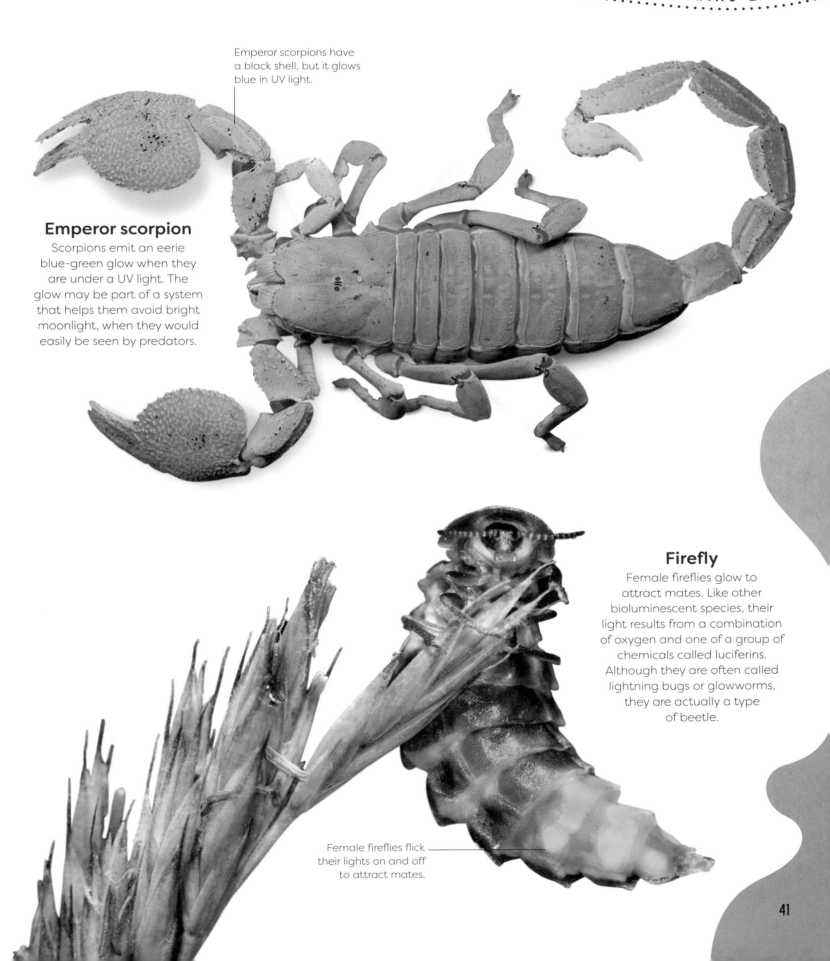

Emperor scorpions have a black shell, but it glows blue in UV light.

Emperor scorpion

Scorpions emit an eerie blue-green glow when they are under a UV light. The glow may be part of a system that helps them avoid bright moonlight, when they would easily be seen by predators.

Firefly

Female fireflies glow to attract mates. Like other bioluminescent species, their light results from a combination of oxygen and one of a group of chemicals called luciferins. Although they are often called lightning bugs or glowworms, they are actually a type of beetle.

Female fireflies flick their lights on and off to attract mates.

41

Glowing sea

On warm nights, the ocean itself sometimes glitters and glows. The blue light is produced by masses of single-celled organisms called dinoflagellates, also known as sea sparkle. Movement in the water, stirred up by a dolphin, swimmer, or breaking waves, sets off a chemical reaction in these tiny life-forms, making them glow.

Leaf insect

These insects are amazing mimics of the leaves around them.

Adult insects always have six legs and a body divided into three parts, but they can still look totally different from each other. They probably come in more shapes and sizes than any other type of animal. Many of them have brilliant camouflage—and none more so than the leaf insects found in tropical rain forests. Every part of these insects has become as leaflike as possible. Their bodies and legs are broad and flat, just like leaves. They are the same shade of green, too. There are even ridges on their bodies that look like leaf ribs and veins. Real leaves often have torn areas or brown spots caused by damage or disease, and some kinds of leaf insect copy these as well.

Leaf insects are also extraordinary for the way they reproduce. The females usually fertilize their own eggs, without the need for males. Because of this, males are very rare. In fact, nearly all leaf insects are female! This unusual form of reproduction can happen in some other insects, as well as in a few reptiles, amphibians, and fish.

Giant Malaysian leaf insect
(Phyllium giganteum)
You will need sharp eyes to spot this insect in the treetops of its rain forest home. It is found in Malaysia.

Like a leaf
The leaf insect's camouflage works best if it stays perfectly still, because if it moves, it might give itself away. When there is a breeze in the forest, though, young leaf insects, called nymphs, sway from side to side to copy the movement of the nearby leaves.

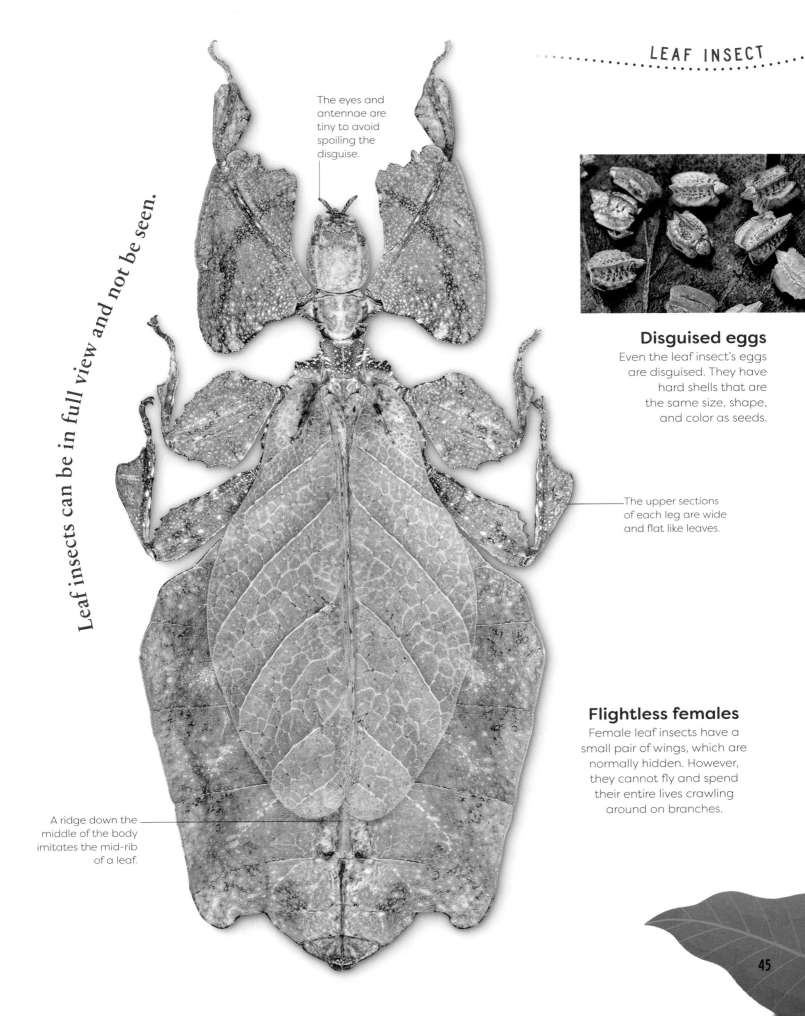

The eyes and antennae are tiny to avoid spoiling the disguise.

Leaf insects can be in full view and not be seen.

The upper sections of each leg are wide and flat like leaves.

A ridge down the middle of the body imitates the mid-rib of a leaf.

Disguised eggs

Even the leaf insect's eggs are disguised. They have hard shells that are the same size, shape, and color as seeds.

Flightless females

Female leaf insects have a small pair of wings, which are normally hidden. However, they cannot fly and spend their entire lives crawling around on branches.

Bumpy skin breaks up the frog's outline.

Mossy frog

In its forest home, this frog is hard to tell apart from real clumps of moss, thanks to the hundreds of lumps and bumps all over its skin, which are in many beautiful shades of green.

Tasseled wobbegong

When this flat shark lies still on the seabed, it appears to be a rock. The frilly skin around its jaws moves in the current like seaweed, hiding it while it waits for prey to come past.

Frills of skin on the wobbegong's chin look like a beard of seaweed.

Camouflage

All kinds of animals use camouflage to disappear. Many of them need to escape the attention of predators, and, in turn, predators have to hide from their prey. Over time, their appearance and behavior have changed in astonishing ways to help them blend in with the world around them.

Mary river turtle
To help it hide in weedy ponds, this Australian turtle lets green algae grow on its head. It can also breathe underwater through its rear end, which allows it to stay submerged for days!

Dead leaf moth
Many moths are the color of dead leaves, complete with lines that imitate veins. This one goes even further, because its wings are curled, too, just like a dried leaf.

Leafy sea dragon
Leafy sea dragons have so many flaps of loose skin that they look more like plants than fish. They also swim in a most unfishlike way, by drifting slowly like bits of seaweed.

Leaf-tailed gecko
This little lizard from Madagascar has a tail like a leaf, and, since its whole body is flattened, it can squish itself against a tree trunk or branch to make itself vanish.

Giant swallowtail caterpillar
Some caterpillars, such as this one of the giant swallowtail butterfly, do an excellent impression of bird poop. No predator wants to eat that, so the caterpillars get left alone.

Northern potoo
The potoo seems to become part of the tree stump it perches on. Its plumage is a perfect match for the bark, and to complete the disguise, it stretches out and shuts its eyes.

Blue tarantula
The spectacular peacock tarantula is huge and has a brilliant blue body. It lives in a small area of forest in India and is critically endangered.

Female jewel tarantulas measure up to 2½ in (6 cm) with their legs at full stretch.

Glittering colors
The jewel tarantula's glittering colors remain a mystery. Scientists believe they probably help it attract a mate.

The entire body is covered in long hair.

Some spiders can see more colors than humans.

Like other tarantulas, this spider's jaws strike downward with a stabbing action.

Brazilian jewel tarantula

The world's most colorful tarantula is as pretty as a butterfly.

Something glitters as it runs across the bark of a tree. It's a spider with the most amazing jewel-like colors. The spider's head is green, its eight legs are pink and blue, and there are patches of red and gold on its body. Called the Brazilian jewel tarantula, it is like no other spider on the planet. Though it looks brightest during the day, this species usually hunts at night, when its prey is most active. Insects and many-legged millipedes are its main targets. To catch them, it hides in the bark of a tree under a trapdoor woven from its own silk and disguised with plant material. When they come near, it pounces.

As with most spiders, the female Brazilian jewel tarantula is bigger than the male, but even she would fit on a playing card. Other tarantulas are much larger, though. Largest of all is the goliath bird spider, which hunts birds, often by climbing trees to snatch them from their nests as they sleep. A big female may have a legspan of 12 in (30 cm) and live up to 35 years.

Brazilian jewel tarantula
(*Typhochlaena seladonia*)
This tarantula can only be seen in the Atlantic Forest, an area of tropical rain forest on the east coast of Brazil. It shares its home with many rare species.

Itchy hairs

Tarantulas don't use their venomous bite to deal with enemies. Instead, their bodies are covered in loosely attached hairs that are incredibly itchy. If a predator attacks, the spiders use their back legs to flick these nasty hairs in the face of their enemy.

Golden-headed lion tamarin

Brazilian jewel
tarantula

49

The smooth shell is the size of a dinner plate.

Many lenses

There are two large eyes made up of 1,000 smaller units, each with a lens and light sensors. Eyes like these are called compound eyes.

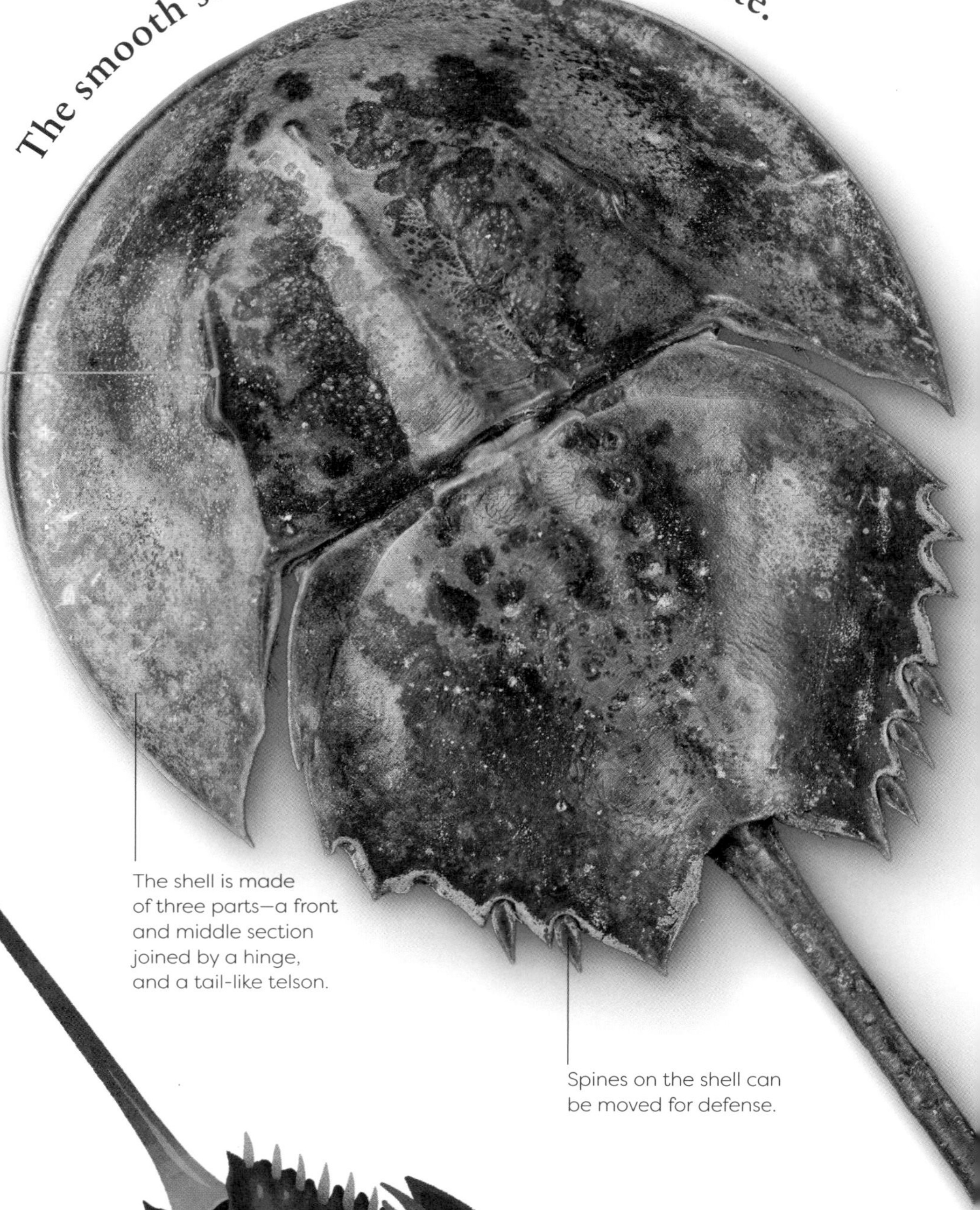

The shell is made of three parts—a front and middle section joined by a hinge, and a tail-like telson.

Spines on the shell can be moved for defense.

Under the shell

Turning a horseshoe crab over reveals its mouthparts and 10 legs, the last pair of which are longer and used to push it along. Behind these are six pairs of flaps that flip up like the pages of a book. The rear five are book gills, used for breathing, and the front pair are used for reproduction.

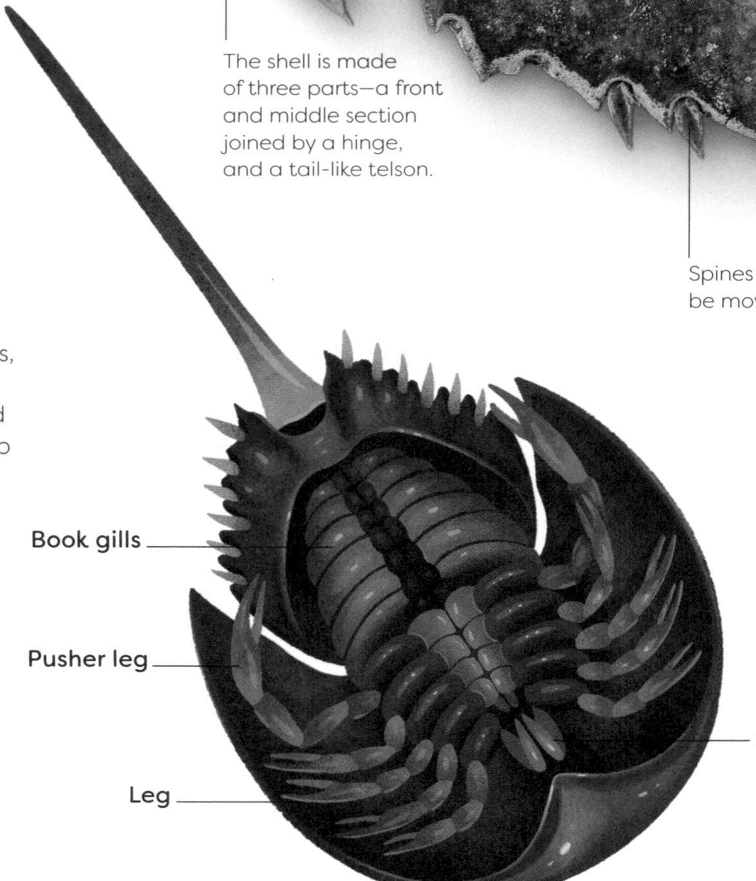

Book gills

Pusher leg

Mouthparts

Leg

Horseshoe crab

Unusual horseshoe crabs appeared on Earth long before the dinosaurs.

We know from fossils that the first horseshoe crabs lived in warm seas 445 million years ago. They survived a time called the Great Dying, when virtually all ocean life became extinct, and are still alive today. They aren't actually crabs, but relatives of spiders and scorpions. At night in May and June, they swarm onto beaches on the highest tides. Often there are so many, their domed shells look like the helmets of an invading army. After mating in the surf, the female horseshoe crabs crawl to the top of the beach and dig pits in the sand for their eggs. They lay as many as 80,000 eggs during several visits. After two weeks, the babies hatch and scuttle down to the ocean.

Horseshoe crabs have bright blue blood that is very sensitive to bacteria. This makes it useful in medicine. Their blood is taken in a lab, then added to human vaccines to check that they are free from bacteria and safe to use. However, some crabs die in the process, so scientists are developing different ways to test vaccines.

Sharp tail

Though the pointed tail, called a telson, appears ferocious, it is not a sting. The horseshoe crab uses it to steer and to turn itself the right way up if it gets flipped upside down.

Atlantic horseshoe crab
(Limulus polyphemus)
These horseshoe crabs are only seen when they come ashore in the spring to breed on the east coast of North America. The rest of the time they live on the ocean floor.

Colorful crustacean

The peacock mantis shrimp has eyes on stalks that can swivel in every direction. This gives it an incredibly wide view of the seabed, and its eyes detect patterns of light no other animal can see. When it locks onto a target, such as a crab or snail, its two clublike arms punch faster than a speeding bullet!

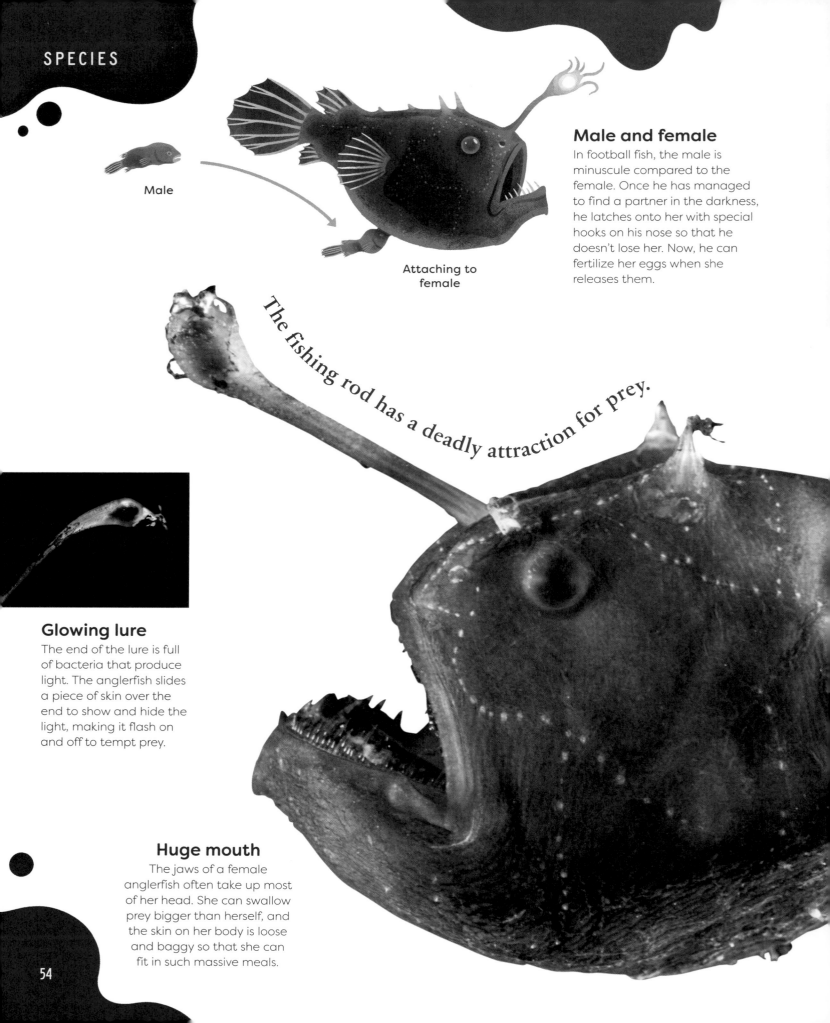

Male

Attaching to female

Male and female

In football fish, the male is minuscule compared to the female. Once he has managed to find a partner in the darkness, he latches onto her with special hooks on his nose so that he doesn't lose her. Now, he can fertilize her eggs when she releases them.

The fishing rod has a deadly attraction for prey.

Glowing lure

The end of the lure is full of bacteria that produce light. The anglerfish slides a piece of skin over the end to show and hide the light, making it flash on and off to tempt prey.

Huge mouth

The jaws of a female anglerfish often take up most of her head. She can swallow prey bigger than herself, and the skin on her body is loose and baggy so that she can fit in such massive meals.

Deep-sea anglerfish

These fierce hunters tempt prey with a glowing bulb on their heads.

Football fish
(Himantolophus)

Female football fish are large and almost spherical, which is how they got their name. Like other deep-sea anglerfish, they soon die if brought to the surface and are rarely captured alive.

Many strange fish live in the sunless depths of the ocean. Very little sunlight reaches farther than 650 ft (200 m) under the surface, and below this is the deep sea. It's a vast and dark world where food is difficult to find, but deep-sea anglerfish have solved this problem. Part of the fin on their backs has turned into a kind of fishing rod, or lure, that dangles in front of their giant mouths. The tip lights up to attract prey, usually other fish or squid. When a victim comes close enough, their jaws snap shut and gulp it down whole.

The female football fish, a type of anglerfish, hunts this way, too, but not the male. He is much smaller and has a very different life. Like prey, he is attracted by the female's light, but avoids her jaws and instead hooks onto her belly. When she releases her eggs, he is ready to fertilize them. Eventually, the male drops off, but in other types of anglerfish, the male's body slowly joins with the female's. Now, he has become a parasite, but the female never needs to find another mate.

Spots on the football fish's body are sensors to detect movement.

Deep-sea species

The deep sea is the largest habitat on the planet, but we know so little about it that most expeditions to the ocean depths discover new animals never seen before. These strange creatures are adapted to life in the dark under the immense pressure of the water above them, and they can look very strange.

Pelican eel

Also called the gulper eel, this fish has stretchy jaws that can swallow huge mouthfuls of water and prey, just like a pelican. It is almost all mouth, with a thin body and stringy tail.

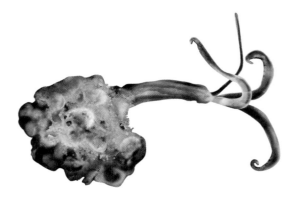

Bone-eating snot flower

This weird creature is not a plant but a deep-sea worm. It sends out roots that drill into the bodies of dead whales lying on the ocean floor and releases acid to digest their bones.

Blobfish

The blobfish has weak bones and hardly any muscle, so it seems to be made of jelly. Being soft and floppy is a great way to survive in the deep sea, where the pressure would crush a shallow-water fish.

Barreleye fish

This fish has upward-facing eyes that look directly above it to try to spot the outlines of prey. The top of its head is see-through, like the bubble visor of an astronaut's helmet.

Dumbo octopus

The dumbo octopus swims by flapping a pair of wide fins on top of its body. The fins look a bit like ears, and the octopus is named after a famous cartoon elephant who flaps his large ears to fly.

Dragonfish

The dragonfish produces red light from its nose to communicate with other dragonfish. No other fish anywhere on Earth is able to create this type of light.

A glowing lure attracts prey into the dragonfish's toothy jaws.

Goblin shark

Thanks to its pointed snout, the goblin shark is one of the spookiest sharks in the ocean! Its long nose is packed with sense organs that pick up the electrical signals made by its prey.

This shark can shoot its jaws forward to snatch prey.

The hatchetfish's flat body and shiny silver scales make it look like an ax blade.

Greater silver hatchetfish

Like many fish in the deep sea, the hatchetfish has organs on its belly that produce blue light. This light matches the weak daylight coming from above and so helps to hide the fish from predators below.

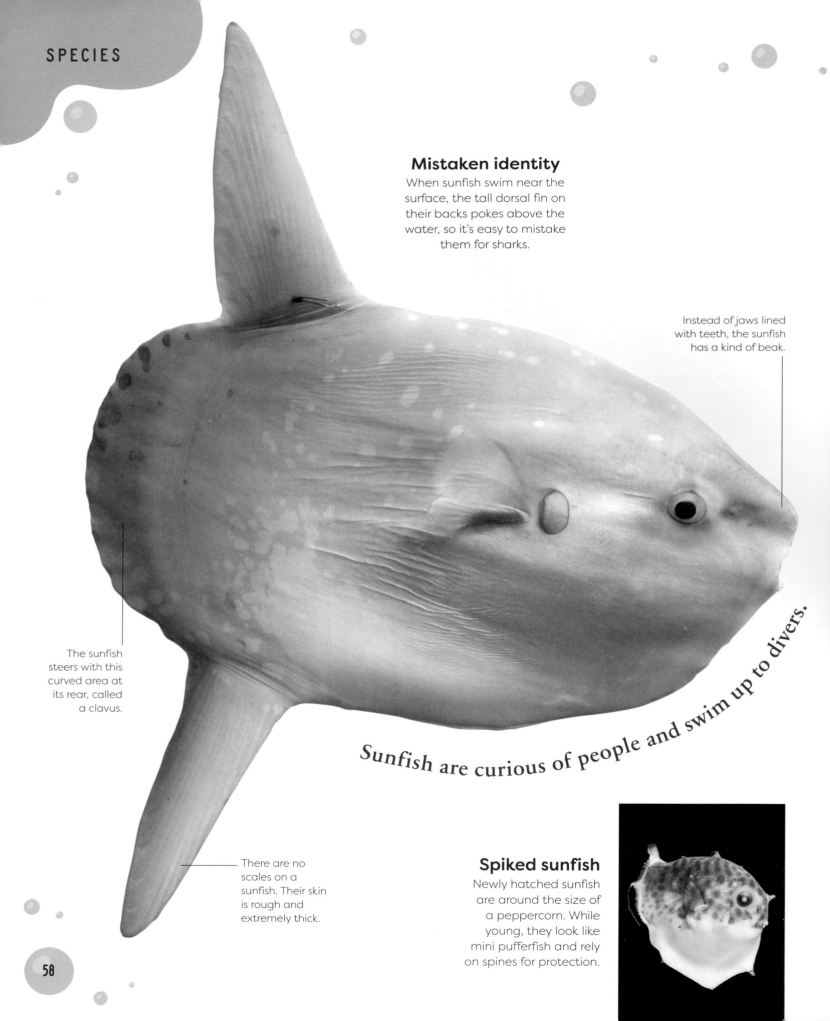

Mistaken identity
When sunfish swim near the surface, the tall dorsal fin on their backs pokes above the water, so it's easy to mistake them for sharks.

Instead of jaws lined with teeth, the sunfish has a kind of beak.

The sunfish steers with this curved area at its rear, called a clavus.

Sunfish are curious of people and swim up to divers.

There are no scales on a sunfish. Their skin is rough and extremely thick.

Spiked sunfish
Newly hatched sunfish are around the size of a peppercorn. While young, they look like mini pufferfish and rely on spines for protection.

Sunfish

Sunfish are gentle giants that glide through the ocean with two huge fins.

Sunfish love to flop onto their sides at the surface of the ocean to enjoy the sun's warmth. This odd behavior is how they got their name. Perhaps it helps them recover after deep dives into cold water to catch jellyfish, their favorite food. Floating among the waves also allows seabirds to peck annoying parasites off their skin. Thanks to their enormous disk-shaped bodies, the sunfish make a bizarre spectacle as they drift along. They have no tail and seem to be just a head with two massive fins!

Adult sunfish often weigh more than a car—the largest ever recorded was as heavy as a full-grown female African elephant. They are easily the world's heaviest bony fish—the only other fish that can be heavier are sharks and their relatives that have just cartilage for a skeleton. Being supersized, sunfish don't have any enemies, but to become so bulky, the babies must grow incredibly fast. They can put on 2 lb (1 kg) a day and finish up being 60 million times heavier than when they hatched! That's a bigger weight gain than any other animal with a backbone.

Ocean sunfish
(Mola mola)
Ocean sunfish swim through warm oceans worldwide. They are spreading north and south into new areas because of ocean warming caused by climate change.

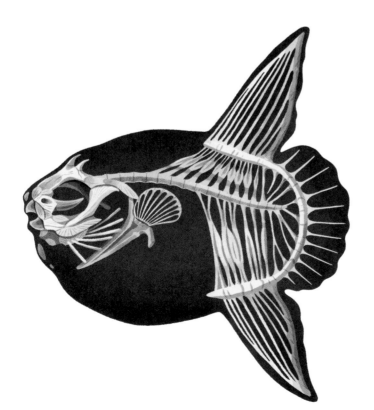

Sunfish skeleton

The reason sunfish can grow so large is because they have an unusual lightweight skeleton. Much of it is not bone, but cartilage, the same material we have in our ears and the front of our nose. Cartilage is strong, yet much lighter than bone.

59

Flatfish

These fish have a pancake-flat body and twisted face.

Some fish living on the ocean floor look as though someone has stepped on them! Their bodies are as flat as the seabed itself, and their bizarre eyes and crooked mouths point upward, toward the ocean's surface. We call these fish flatfish, and there are hundreds of different kinds, including many caught for food, such as plaice, halibut, sole, and flounder. They spend the day motionless on the sand or mud, hoping no predators will spot them. At night, they move around the seabed in search of prey—or wait for it to stumble upon them.

The amazing thing about flatfish such as the European flounder is that their larvae start off like regular fish and swim upright. In time, however, they move to the ocean floor and experience a radical change. Their bodies flatten, their mouths twist, and one eye migrates across the head to join the other. In some flatfish, the left eye moves; in others it is the right eye. The side that will end up lying on the seafloor turns white, but the upper side develops a pattern for camouflage.

European flounder
(Platichthys flesus)
This flatfish lives along the coasts of the eastern Atlantic Ocean and the Mediterranean Sea. It rests on the seabed with its eyeless side facing down.

Total transformation
Soon after hatching, the flounder begins its transformation. Its skull bones bend, its jaws are pushed out of alignment, and its fins change shape. Usually, it is the left eye that begins slowly moving across the top of its head to meet the right, but sometimes it is the other way around.

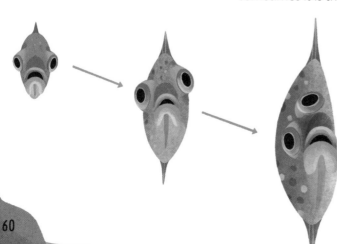

A flat tail helps push the fish along as it ripples its body to swim.

Flatfish have both eyes on one side of their heads.

On this flounder, the left eye has moved over to the right side of the head.

Dramatic change

Color-changing cells in the flounder's skin alter its appearance in seconds to match the seabed on which it lies. It can become darker or lighter and change its pattern.

A flattened fin reaches from the head to the tail along each side of the fish.

Clever camouflage

When the flounder buries itself in the sandy seabed, only its mouth and eyes poke out. Unless you look very closely, you would never know a fish was there.

Blind cave fish

Life in the dark means this fish can do without eyes.

Imagine living in a cave where it is forever dark and there's little food. You might think no animals would be found in these environments, but cave animals include spiders, shrimp, and fish. The blind cave fish, or Mexican tetra, which lives in underground caves in Mexico, is a perfect example. It looks very different from its relatives at the surface. Over many generations, it has become very pale and some no longer have eyes! There is no need for eyes in their sunless world, and they save energy by not having to grow them.

Because it can't see its surroundings, the blind cave fish is instead amazingly sensitive to movement. It feels its way through underground pools by sensing tiny changes in water pressure. It also makes clicking sounds, probably to home in on food. The clicks create little pulses of water that bounce off objects, and the fish picks up these ripples as they return to learn where everything is. The fish in each cave have developed their own style of clicks, as if speaking a different language.

These fish are small enough to fit in the palm of your hand.

Blind cave fish
(Astyanax mexicanus)
Eyeless forms of this fish live in flooded caves in Mexico. They eat small cave animals and scraps of food washed into the caves by heavy rain.

Scales grow over the eye sockets, which show as dark smudges.

No eyes

With eyes

Two types

After millions of years living in the dark, groups of this fish have become eyeless and very pale. However, groups that live in pools and streams at the surface still have eyes and bright silver bodies. The two types of fish are the same species.

This fish swims around in total darkness.

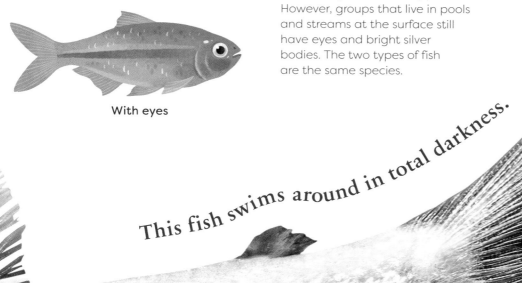

Slime armor

Like many fish, the blind cave fish is covered in a thick layer of slime that stops harmful bacteria from growing on it.

The body is pink or cream in color.

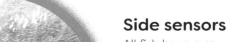

Side sensors

All fish have a row of sensors along the middle of both sides of their bodies, called lateral lines. These detect movement and pressure changes in the water to help the fish explore their surroundings.

63

Horn shark

Female horn sharks lay unique eggs with beautiful spiral cases.

Most female fish release their eggs into the water, where the males fertilize them. Sharks, however, mate like mammals. The females often still lay eggs afterward though, rather than give birth to babies. Horn sharks, for example, mate after a short chase over the seabed. Having mated, the female shark quickly swims away, and over the next few months, she will lay 20 or so eggs. Thanks to their olive-green color and tough spiral cases, they look extraordinary. The unusual shape might remind you of a drill bit or screw. Most shark eggs are rectangular and flat, so why are these eggs so different? The answer is that the spiral design helps to wedge them under boulders or in crevices among rocks. The female horn shark picks up her eggs in her mouth and pushes them tightly into these hiding places. This makes it harder for predators to eat the eggs and stops the current and tides from tugging them away. It can take up to 10 months for the embryo inside to develop, so the egg needs to be securely anchored in place.

Mermaid's purse
The empty, dry egg cases of sharks are often found washed up on beaches. They are known as mermaids' purses.

The spiral edge wedges the egg case into gaps between rocks.

Horn shark
(*Heterodontus francisci*)
This small shark is found along North America's west coast, from California south to Mexico. It preys on sea snails and other shelled animals, crunching them up with its grinding teeth.

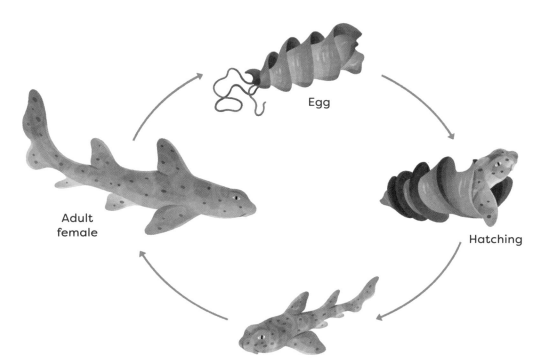

Egg

Adult
female

Hatching

Young

Shark life cycle

After mating, the female horn shark lays her eggs in batches of two throughout the spring and summer. Each egg contains a single embryo. The baby shark, called a pup, hatches around 10 months later by chewing its way out of the egg case before swimming off.

The egg case is unlike anything produced by any other animal.

Each egg case is around 4 in (10 cm) long.

Leathery shell

A freshly laid egg has a soft case at first, but it soon hardens and turns leathery, which helps to keep the pup inside safe.

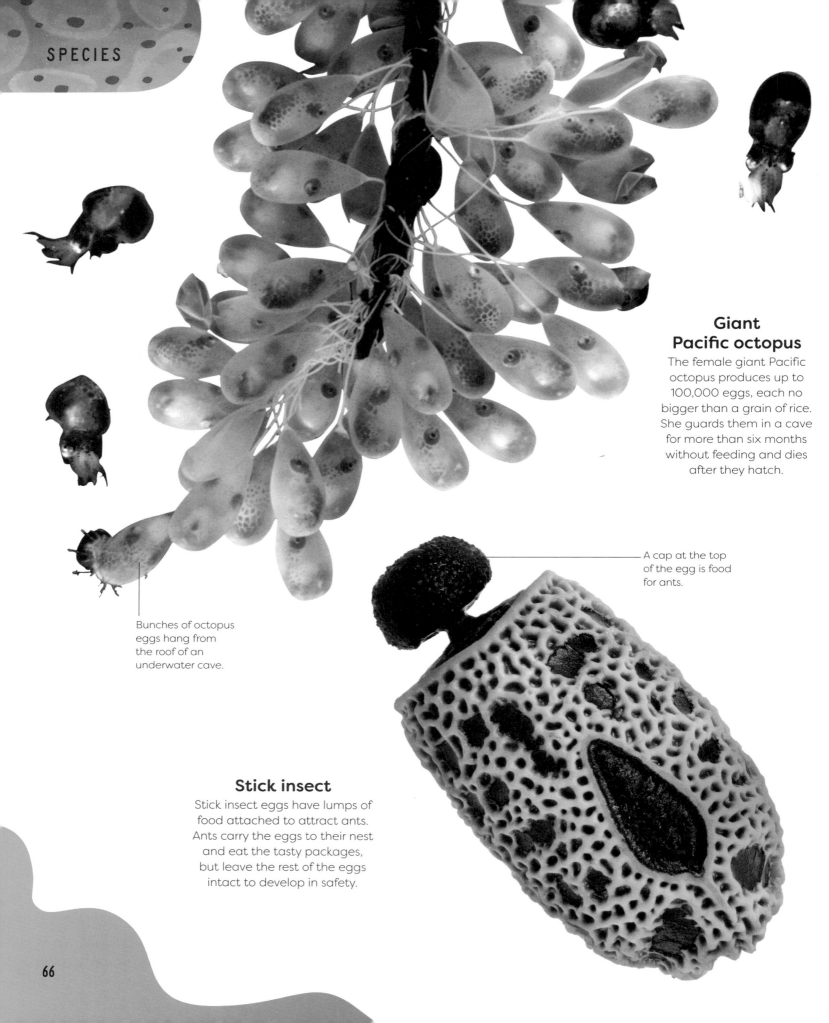

Giant Pacific octopus

The female giant Pacific octopus produces up to 100,000 eggs, each no bigger than a grain of rice. She guards them in a cave for more than six months without feeding and dies after they hatch.

Bunches of octopus eggs hang from the roof of an underwater cave.

A cap at the top of the egg is food for ants.

Stick insect

Stick insect eggs have lumps of food attached to attract ants. Ants carry the eggs to their nest and eat the tasty packages, but leave the rest of the eggs intact to develop in safety.

Eggs

When we think of an egg, we often picture a chicken's egg. However, every bird lays different eggs, and birds are not the only egg-laying animals—in fact, 99 percent of animals produce eggs. Their eggs vary enormously in appearance and how they develop.

Ratfish

Female ratfish, also called chimaeras, are related to sharks and lay eggs with leathery cases. The eggs stay attached to the female on threads for several days before falling to the seabed.

Mosquito

The eggs of some mosquitoes float on the surface of puddles and ponds. They cling together to form a waterproof raft whose ends curve upward to keep the raft afloat.

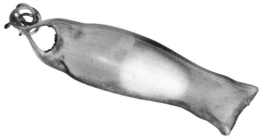

Catshark

These sharks lay strange egg cases with stiff threads at the corners. The threads get tangled in seaweed and hold each case tight while the baby shark finishes growing.

Assassin bug

Female assassin bugs deposit their eggs on the underside of leaves. Some carefully suspend their eggs in amazingly neat towers, all facing in the same direction with their caps on one side.

Southern cassowary

Cassowaries are flightless birds that lay huge green eggs, each as heavy as three oranges. The female lays them, but it is the male's job to incubate them until they are ready to hatch.

Praying mantis

These insects cover their clutch of eggs in special foam as they are laid, which hardens into a gray shell, called an ootheca. The shell stops the eggs inside from drying out and protects them from predators.

Axolotl

When injured, an axolotl regrows its body parts and internal organs.

Mexico's axolotl gets its name from an old Aztec word meaning "water servant." It's a peculiar kind of salamander and may remind you of a giant tadpole or an eel with legs. Like other salamanders, it starts life in fresh water, but unlike them, it never leaves. When it reaches adulthood at about two years old, it keeps the features it had as a larva, including an extra wide, flat tail and six frilly gills for breathing underwater.

The unusual axolotl also has an incredible superpower. If it is attacked, any lost or damaged limbs and gills will grow back. It will even grow a whole new tail, complete with muscles and spinal cord. Incredibly, it can also rebuild its eyes, lungs, and kidneys, as well as parts of its heart and brain! The repairs only take a few weeks and leave no scars. Scientists are studying this amazing amphibian to learn its secrets. They found that we have the same genes that enable the axolotl to regenerate; it's just that our bodies don't use them the same way. Maybe one day their discoveries will enable humans to regrow limbs, too.

In danger
Today, the last few wild axolotls live in a lake on the outskirts of Mexico City, where they are threatened by pollution and new types of fish that have been released by people.

Feathery gills
The axolotl's gills absorb most of the oxygen it needs from the water, and they also get rid of the waste carbon dioxide from its body.

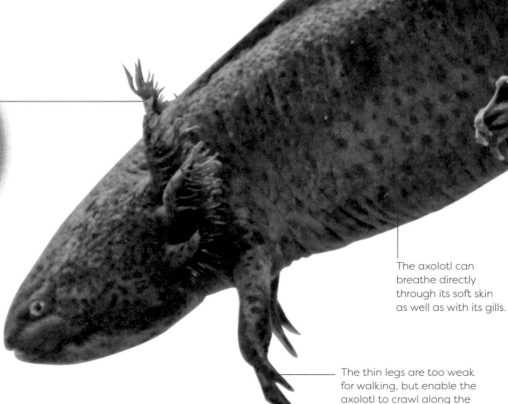

The axolotl can breathe directly through its soft skin as well as with its gills.

The thin legs are too weak for walking, but enable the axolotl to crawl along the bottom of a lake.

Axolotl
(*Ambystoma mexicanum*)
Wild axolotls in Mexico are greenish gray or black. In tanks, you often see pale pink ones, which have been bred.

A flattened tail acts like a fin to help the axolotl swim.

The axolotl can replace lost limbs over and over again.

Growing up

Most salamanders hatch from an egg into a larva, then change into an adult in a process called metamorphosis. Axolotls become adults without going through metamorphosis and hold onto their larval features into adulthood. This is known as neoteny and is very rare.

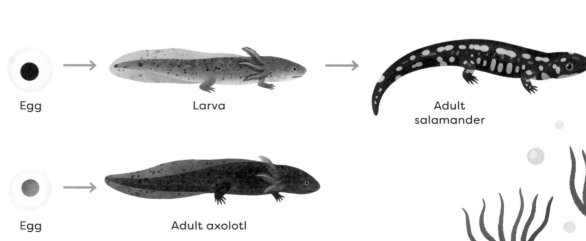

Egg → Larva → Adult salamander

Egg → Adult axolotl

69

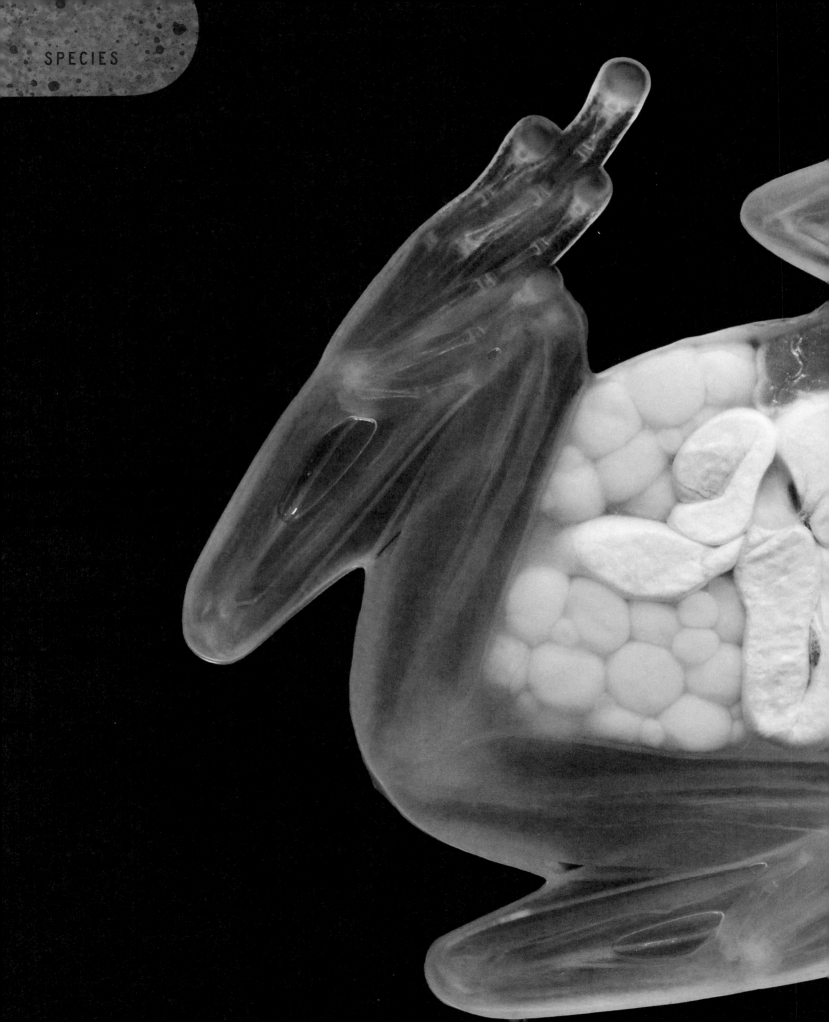

See-through frog

Glass frogs have unusual camouflage that works like a kind of invisibility cloak. Their skin and muscles are see-through, and their organs reflect light, so they seem to vanish into thin air. Their blood is still red, but when resting, the frogs can hide it by diverting red blood cells to the liver.

71

The shoebill has a tuft of feathers at the back of its head.

Water carrier

Shoebills nest in the open, so their chicks risk overheating in the fierce sun. The parents carry water in their mighty beaks to soak the young and cool them down.

The shoebill stands as still as a statue as it waits for prey.

Although usually quiet, the shoebill can clack its beak rapidly to make a distinctive sound.

Sharp beak

A sharp hook, called a nail, at the tip of the upper half of the shoebill's beak gives it a strong grip on slippery fish.

Shoebill

This huge bird has a beak like a giant shoe.

A gray-feathered giant strides across a muddy swamp. On its stiltlike legs, it is as tall as a seven-year-old child. The heavy bird's enormously long toes allow it to walk on floating plants without sinking. But its bizarre beak is what catches your eye—no other species has a beak quite like this. It is the shape of a traditional wooden clog and gives the bird its name: shoebill.

The shoebill's unusual beak allows it to catch a variety of large animals living in the swamp. Its favorite prey is the African lungfish, which has a slippery, eel-like body as long as your arm. Fishing is difficult in the murky swamp water, but the shoebill waits motionless for half an hour or more, looking for any slight ripple that might reveal its prey. Often it doesn't even see the fish and just feels something move with its feet. It then lunges forward and plunges its beak into the water to seize its meal. The shoebill also hunts turtles, water snakes, and young crocodiles. Big crocodiles, however, like to prey on young shoebills!

Shoebill
(*Balaeniceps rex*)
The shoebill lives in vast swamps in Central and East Africa. Other names for it include "whalebill" and "whale-headed stork."

Swallowing prey
Before the shoebill can swallow fish, it has to turn them headfirst in its beak, so their scales don't get stuck in its throat. Its eyes have a third eyelid that closes to prevent injury as the wriggling prey thrashes around.

73

American flamingo

Unlike any other bird, a flamingo holds its beak upside down to feed. The bird stands in a shallow lake with its beak slightly open and uses it to sieve tiny algae and shrimp from the water.

Flamingos hatch with a straight bill, but it soon develops a bend.

The beak is hollow inside, so is much lighter than it looks.

Keel-billed toucan

This bird from Central and South America has a dazzling beak around a third as long as its body. Though the beak might appear to be clumsy, it is actually a fantastic tool that allows the bird to feed on fruits and nuts.

Beaks

Ancient birds developed from dinosaurs, which had beaks full of teeth, but over millions of years the teeth disappeared. Birds now have beaks, or bills, in a mind-boggling variety of shapes and sizes to help them grab, stab, tear, crack, tweezer, or sift their food.

Black skimmer
Each half of the skimmer's beak is a different length. It flies low over water with the longer half just under the surface, and whenever it feels a fish, its beak slams shut.

Northern brown kiwi
Most birds have nostrils near their head. However, New Zealand's kiwis have them at the tip of their long beak so they can sniff out worms as they probe the forest soil.

Common crossbill
This forest bird uses its peculiar beak like a pair of pliers. Because the ends of the beak cross over, it can insert them between the scales of pine cones to pull out the seeds inside.

Wrybill
When a wrybill faces you, its beak always bends to the left. This unique quirk enables it to reach under pebbles in streams to find insects and small fish to eat.

Roseate spoonbill
Spoonbills possess an extraordinary beak that is long, flat, and rounded at the end, like a giant spoon. They sweep it around in shallow, muddy water to feel for shrimp and other prey.

Sulawesi wrinkled hornbill
Hornbills have an extension on top of their beaks, called a casque, which, like the rest of the beak, is hollow. It helps the birds to attract a mate and increases the volume of their loud barks.

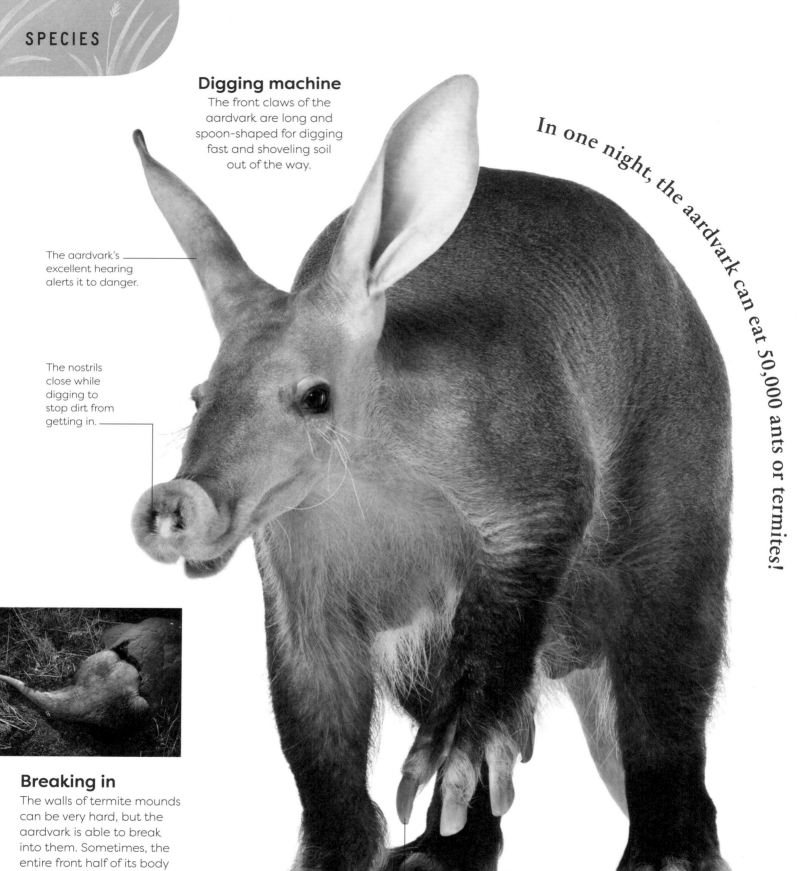

Digging machine
The front claws of the aardvark are long and spoon-shaped for digging fast and shoveling soil out of the way.

The aardvark's excellent hearing alerts it to danger.

The nostrils close while digging to stop dirt from getting in.

In one night, the aardvark can eat 50,000 ants or termites!

Breaking in
The walls of termite mounds can be very hard, but the aardvark is able to break into them. Sometimes, the entire front half of its body disappears inside!

There are four toes on the front feet. The back feet have five.

Aardvark

The aardvark seems to be assembled from the parts of many other animals.

You are looking at perhaps the oddest animal in all of Africa. Its name, aardvark, means "earth pig," but the aardvark is so unusual, scientists have decided it does not have any close relatives and belongs in a family of its own. Its body and tail resemble a giant rat, but its pink skin and snuffly nose are like a pig, and it has a donkey's big, pointed ears. The animal also reminds people of anteaters from South America, because like them, its snout is long and tubelike. That's not surprising, because it eats the same food—ants and antlike insects called termites. At night, the aardvark leaves its burrow to break into their nests with its powerful claws. It digs fast, sending soil everywhere, and is a fast eater, too, using its super-sticky tongue to lick up thousands of the creepy-crawlies. Soldier ants and termites swarm out to bite and sting the aardvark, but, thanks to its tough skin, it barely feels a thing. If a large predator comes along, the aardvark is quickly able to dig a new burrow into which it can escape.

Aardvark
(Orycteropus afer)
The aardvark can be found in much of Africa south of the Sahara Desert. It is nocturnal and its eyesight is poor, so it relies on its superb sense of smell and hearing to get around.

Eye socket

Nose

Teeth

Unusual teeth

Aardvarks have very strange teeth. There are just 20 of them, all at the back of the jaw. They lack roots and enamel—the hard outer layer of our teeth—and never stop growing. Most of the time, aardvarks don't chew their food at all.

Pink fairy armadillo

This is the world's only mammal with a bright pink "shell."

Armadillos are built like tanks. The upper part of their bodies have thick armor, made from many flat pieces of bone with an even tougher layer of horn on top. It's an excellent defense, but the pink fairy armadillo uses its armor for something else. Around the size of a gerbil, it burrows in warm plains, where staying the right temperature is a problem. The sandy ground can be painfully hot by day and bitterly cold by night. So, this little armadillo has turned its armored "shell" into a radiator. During the day, it pumps blood into the shell, which heats up. The shell releases the heat and the armadillo cools down. At night, the armadillo does the opposite—it empties its shell of blood to stop itself from losing heat and getting cold.

Why, though, is the pink fairy armadillo such an unusual color? Because it lives underground, it does not need much melanin— the dark pigment that gives protection from sunburn. This means you can partly see the blood showing through its skin and shell, which makes it pink.

Armadillo armor is connected by skin and moves at the joints, like the jointed shell of a lobster or shrimp.

Pink fairy armadillo
(*Chlamyphorus truncatus*)
The pink fairy armadillo lives in Argentina and survives on a diet of ants and a few plants. It is now rare and may be endangered.

Large front claws can dig through the sandy soil with ease.

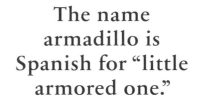

Flat plate

The armadillo's rear end is round and flat, with a fringe of hair at the top. The top half of it is protected by armor.

The name armadillo is Spanish for "little armored one."

This armadillo has a club-shaped tail.

Sand swimming

The pink fairy armadillo digs so fast with its powerful claws, it appears to be swimming through the sand. A pointed head makes tunneling easier. It compacts the sand behind it with its flat rear end so the grains don't fall into the tunnel.

There are 11 pairs of wiggly pink tentacles around this mole's nose.

Powerful paws
The mole digs with its powerful front paws. They are big and broad, with five thick claws, and are turned outward to shovel soil out of the way.

The mole's shoulders are massive and muscular for digging.

The mole's fur lies flat in any direction, so it doesn't stick up when the mole moves down tunnels.

Poor vision
It looks as if the mole doesn't have eyes, but they are just very small. It can barely see and is only able to tell light from dark.

80

Star-nosed mole

Thanks to its nose tentacles, this animal is a super-speedy hunter.

The star-nosed mole could win the prize for oddest-looking mammal in the world. It is roughly the size of a hamster and looks much like other moles, except for one thing. Just look at its nose! At the end, a bunch of 22 pink tentacles wriggle nonstop. They are the mole's "star," an ultrasensitive organ that it uses to feel around and scan its surroundings, like a hand and eye combined.

Being a mole, this fabulous creature spends its life digging tunnels underground. The tentacles in its star constantly check the soil for prey, mostly earthworms and insect grubs. They are stuffed with 100,000 nerve endings that fire vast amounts of data at the mole's brain. As fast as you can blink, the mole locates an object, decides if it is a tasty worm or grub, gobbles it up, and starts looking for the next meal. The whole operation takes a quarter of a second, which makes the star-nosed mole the fastest feeder of any animal. It can also hunt in water by blowing bubbles through its nose and then inhaling them to sniff out prey.

Star-nosed mole
(Condylura cristata)
The star-nosed mole lives in Canada and the eastern US. It digs in the wet soil of swamps and beside streams and ponds, and is the only mole able to swim.

Worm detector

As the mole digs, it presses its star organ against the sides of its tunnel many times a second. The tentacles feel tiny vibrations and changes in pressure in the soil. When the mole detects a worm moving, it seizes the prey in its teeth.

Noses

Animal noses may look strange to us, but they are complex organs that do many important things. They can be adapted for smelling food, catching prey, or attracting breeding partners—sometimes by helping the animal to make loud noises. And, of course, mammals use their noses for breathing, too.

Horned anole

These rare forest lizards are named after the male's spectacular pointed snout. Unlike a horn, it bends enough for him to move it up and down, probably to impress females.

Greater spear-nosed bat

You can't miss the pointed flap of skin, called a nose leaf, on this bat's face. The bat uses it to aim blasts of high-pitched squeaks, which is how it locates its insect prey.

Saiga

The saiga antelope wanders over grasslands in Central Asia, where its massive nose has two essential jobs to do. It filters dirt from the dusty air in summer and it warms up the cold air in winter.

Black-and-rufous sengi

Sengis are tiny African mammals that, surprisingly, are related to elephants. They have long, flexible noses like miniature trunks, which twitch nonstop to sniff out insects, their favorite food.

Proboscis monkey

The male of this species owns a bulbous nose so big it often hangs over his mouth. The larger and droopier it is, the louder his mating calls and the more attractive he will be to females.

Giant anteater

This animal has an astonishingly long snout, perfect for poking into ant and termite nests. Inside is an equally long tongue that is very sticky and can flick in and out twice a second to lick up the insects.

In addition to its eyes, the hammerhead's nostrils are found on each side of its head.

Scalloped hammerhead shark

This spectacular shark uses its T-shaped head to scan the ocean floor. The huge surface creates space for many sensors, which detect smells, tastes, and the weak electrical signals made by prey—stingrays are a particular favorite.

Higher-ranking males have the brightest noses.

Mandrill

Male mandrills are the world's largest monkeys—and the most colorful. Their magnificent red and blue noses are offset by purple eyebrows, red lips, white whiskers, and golden beards.

CHAPTER 2

Behavior

Plants and animals can do the most bizarre and unexpected things. For example, there is a plant that can come back from the dead, a seal that inflates balloons on its head, and there are lizards that squirt blood from their eyes. Animals may behave like this from the moment they are born—this is called instinctive behavior. Or they may pick up their odd habits by copying those around them, which is called learned behavior.

Dry

Rehydrated

Network of veins

Spikemoss stems have veins to carry water, food, and minerals around the plant. True moss has a much simpler structure and lacks veins.

Back to life

Months without rain dry out the spikemoss and turn it into a tight brown ball. Within hours of a sudden downpour, its roots and stems have taken up water and the plant uncurls. Its leaves then turn from brown to green again.

Scaly leaves

The stems are covered in hard green lumps, which are unusual flat leaves called scales. They form a neat pattern all over the surface.

As if by magic, the plant revives in front of your eyes.

86

As the plant revives, each stem begins to unfurl from the center.

Resurrecting plant

In dry spells, this plant shrivels up, but a splash of water returns it to life.

To resurrect something means to bring it back from the dead. Incredibly, this is what the resurrection plant appears to do! It grows in deserts, where long periods without a drop of rain are common. In these parched conditions, the ground is baked as hard as rock and the plant shrivels up completely. It dries to a crisp and curls into a brown ball. Yet it does not actually die, it is merely resting. Even though it has lost virtually all of its water, it can wait like this for many months—or several years, if need be. When rain comes, the effect is instant. The plant pumps water around its stems and springs back to life as if nothing had happened.

The resurrection plant's other name is spikemoss, and it does look a bit like moss. It is an ancient type of plant—fossils have shown us that spikemosses first appeared around 300 million years ago, when the Earth was covered in swampy forests. Like ferns, which also flourished at this time, spikemosses reproduce with microscopic specks called spores, instead of seeds.

Spikemoss is a small plant and grows close to the ground.

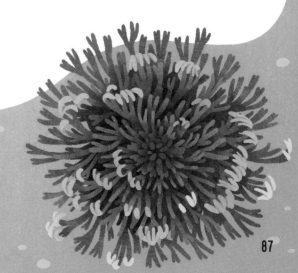

Resurrection plant
(Selaginella lepidophylla)
This spikemoss grows in the Chihuahuan Desert in Mexico, but spikemosses can also be found in other dry habitats, damp forests, and rocky mountains.

Jumping beans

These seeds leap around wildly as if under a spell—and have a secret inside.

With a sudden jolt, a seed jumps off the sandy ground and lands a short distance away. It does it again, and keeps jumping for several more minutes. Has the seed somehow come to life? Not quite—the weird leaping is down to a moth caterpillar living in the seed. It has tied itself to the inside of the seed using silk threads, and by jerking its body it makes the seed move. Many people have puzzled over the mysterious spectacle of "jumping beans," as seeds like these are known. One theory is that the caterpillars make their seeds jump to frighten off any animals that try to eat the seeds—and the unfortunate caterpillars inside. However, a more likely explanation is that this behavior is how they escape the full force of the hot sun. By moving their seeds, the caterpillars can find a cool and shady spot where they are not at risk of drying out. When the caterpillar is ready, it chews an exit hole in the seed wall but remains inside to transform into an adult moth. Only once it has become a moth does it finally leave.

Jumping bean tree
(*Sebastiania pavoniana*)
Most jumping beans come from this type of small tree in Mexico, but jumping bean moth caterpillars also use the seeds of a few other plants in Central America.

Moth life cycle
The female moth lays her eggs in the part of the flower that will become a seed pod. When the caterpillars hatch, they each begin to eat the inside of one seed. Even when the seed falls to the ground, the caterpillar continues to live inside. Eventually, the caterpillar turns into a pupa and the adult moth emerges a few weeks later.

Hidden caterpillar

The moth caterpillar, or larva, is a white grub with strong jaws for gnawing into the seed. It secures itself with a harness made of silk threads.

Every twitch of the caterpillar makes the seed jump.

The seed is packed with protein, so it makes a nutritious meal for a caterpillar.

Seed harvest

Jumping beans have become popular as souvenirs. In Mexico, millions are gathered for sale each year.

Each seed pod is made of three parts, which separate when they fall from the tree.

89

Color change

Octopuses have special skin cells packed with pigments that create visual effects like the pixels in a digital screen. To change color, they change the shape of these cells.

Octopuses are the smartest invertebrates on Earth.

Octopus arms are super stretchy, thanks to their powerful muscles and lack of bones.

Each arm feels and tastes its surroundings with thousands of chemical sensors.

Caterpillar or snake?

The caterpillar of the spicebush swallowtail butterfly copies a snake to scare birds away. It can even pop out an orange structure that looks like a snake's forked tongue.

90

Octopus in disguise

The mimic octopus does excellent impressions of other animals.

If you want to frighten your enemies so they leave you alone, pretending to be something more dangerous than you are is a smart tactic. Many animals do it, including caterpillars that copy snakes, moths that imitate wasps, and harmless frogs that look exactly like poisonous ones, but the mimic octopus is the master. It can disguise itself as a variety of species and easily switch between them. It changes both its color and shape to appear like a number of dangerous creatures that are either venomous or have toxic flesh, such as lionfish, stingrays, sea snakes, jellyfish, and a kind of flatfish called the zebra sole. The octopus does not just imitate their appearance, but their behavior, too. For example, when copying the sole, it lies flat on the seabed, just like the sole does. The mimic octopus also copies animals that are not really that dangerous, such as crabs. Why would it do that? Pretending to be a harmless crab may be a clever way to fool its prey. As a victim comes closer, the octopus snatches its meal!

Mimic octopus
(*Thaumoctopus mimicus*)
Scientists did not know about this little octopus, which lives in the Indian and Pacific oceans, until it was discovered in 1998.

Copycat
To appear like a banded sea snake, the octopus folds in six of its arms and stretches out the other two in a long line. It imitates a lionfish by spreading all eight arms around its body like fins. To copy the zebra sole, it flattens itself on the seafloor in the shape of a fish.

Banded
sea snake

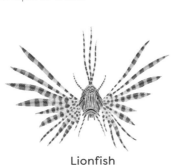

Lionfish

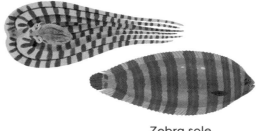

Zebra sole

Poop armor

The larvae of some beetles hide behind a shield
made out of their own waste products. Instead of just
dumping the poop on leaves, these lily beetle larvae
carefully keep it to smear all over their bodies. It may
seem disgusting, but it keeps the larvae safe—
no predator wants to eat them!

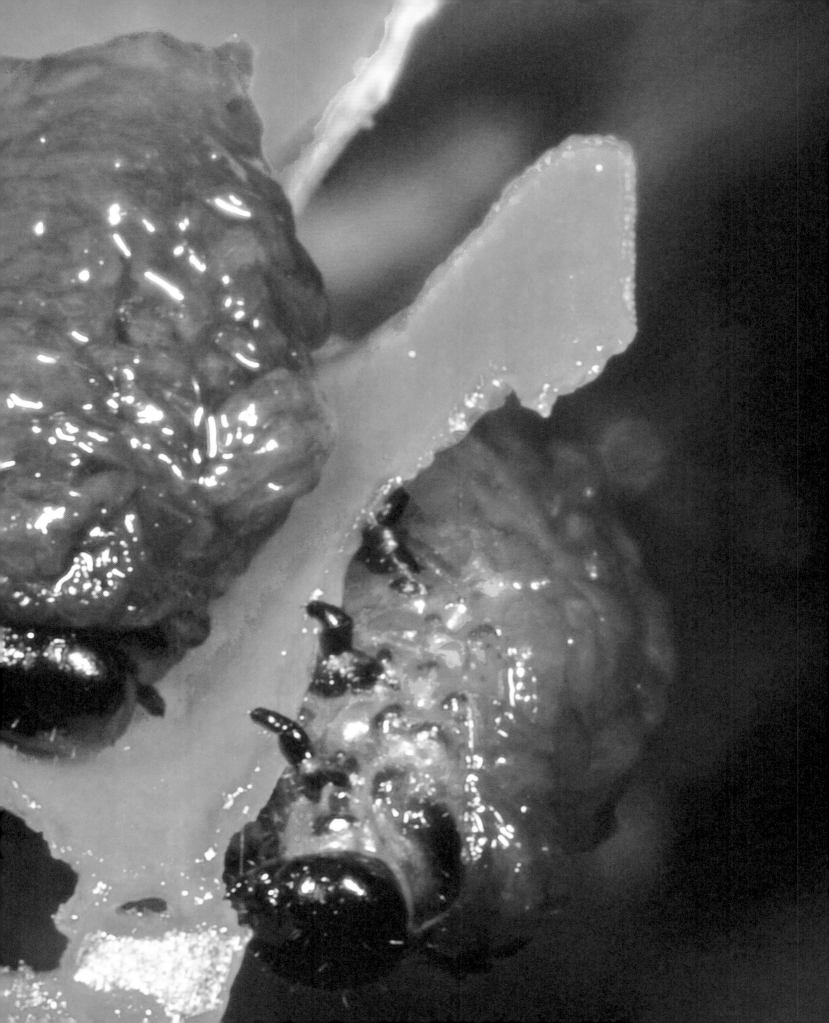

Cooking spider

Some spiders barbecue their prey on the hot sand of deserts.

We once thought that we were the only species that could cook. Cooking doesn't just give food a nice taste, but it also makes meals easier to digest and kills bacteria and parasites that might be growing in it. The ability to light fires to cook food is a major reason humans became successful and spread all over the planet. It turns out, however, that we are not alone—a few spiders are cooks, too!

Spoor spiders live in deserts, where the sand reaches 158°F (70°C) in the afternoon. That's hot enough to sizzle flesh, and these spiders know it. As the day heats up, the female spiders, which are much bigger than the males, dig into the sand to escape the sun. Each hides in her own burrow with a lid made from silk and sand—now all she has to do is wait. When a passing ant walks over the burrow, the spider grabs it and holds its body on the scorching sand at the surface, like meat on a grill, while she stays safe in her tunnel. It doesn't take long for the sun to do its work.

Spoor spiders
(Seothyra)
There are around a dozen different types of spoor spider, all found in the sandy deserts of southern Africa.

Cooking an ant
A female spoor spider prepares her burrow and adds a silk tripwire at its entrance. She takes one end of it down into the burrow to alert her to a passing ant. When she feels movement, she rushes up to seize the ant and holds it against the burning sand.

1. The spider digs a burrow under a lid.

2. When an ant walks past, the spider runs up to it.

3. The ant is held against the hot sand.

A female spider can cook ants twice her size.

Silk is produced by fingerlike spinners at the rear of the body.

This spider is covered in grains of sand.

The spider seizes prey in a pair of leglike structures called palps.

Hot dinner

The ants that these spiders eat also make use of the blistering sand. They feed on the bodies of other insects that have died in the baking heat.

Buried eggs

Female maleo birds bury their eggs in warm sand heated by volcanic activity or the sun's rays. The heat incubates the eggs, so they don't have to!

95

Spider barricade

This spider blocks its enemies with its heavily armored rear.

Spiders are famous for their fabulous silk webs—but spinning webs is not the only way they catch prey. Some chase down prey like wolves, and many dig burrows in the ground where they wait for insects to fall in. Most of the burrowing spiders add a trapdoor at the top, made from soil or sand bound together with their silk. The trapdoor hides the burrow from prey and keeps out predators as well. However, the Chinese hourglass spider also uses its massive back end to block its burrow! This part of its body is extremely tough and flattened into a plate, which, since it is circular, plugs the entrance. With its burrow barricade in place, the spider is safe.

The Chinese hourglass spider's enemies include centipedes and bigger spiders, but the worst is a wasp. The female wasp is a parasite and expert at hunting spiders. She stings her eight-legged victims to paralyze them, then feeds them to her larvae. Luckily for the Chinese hourglass spider, its barricade is strong enough to fend off her jaws and sting.

Tough rump
If in danger, Australia's wombat dives into its burrow and blocks the entrance with its rear end. Thick layers of skin, fur, and fat protect its rear and keep enemies out.

The armored plate has a grooved pattern.

Chinese hourglass spider
(*Cyclocosmia ricketti*)
As far as we know, this spider lives only in a few provinces of southern China. It has become very rare and in recent years has been seen just a handful of times.

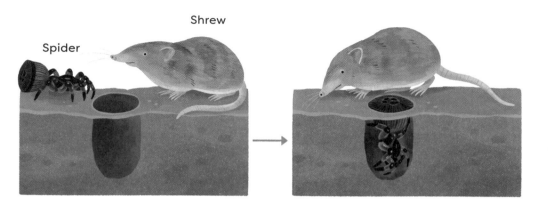

Shrew

Spider

Quick getaway

Meeting a shrew could be a deadly situation for the Chinese hourglass spider, but it escapes by racing down its burrow headfirst. The hard plate on the end of its body seals the opening like a cork in a bottle—and the defeated shrew goes hungry.

The spider's tough rear end fits its burrow entrance perfectly.

Ambush predators

Burrowing spiders are patient hunters that sit tight in their tunnels until vibrations in the ground tell them that an ant, beetle, or some other prey is approaching. Then, they pounce!

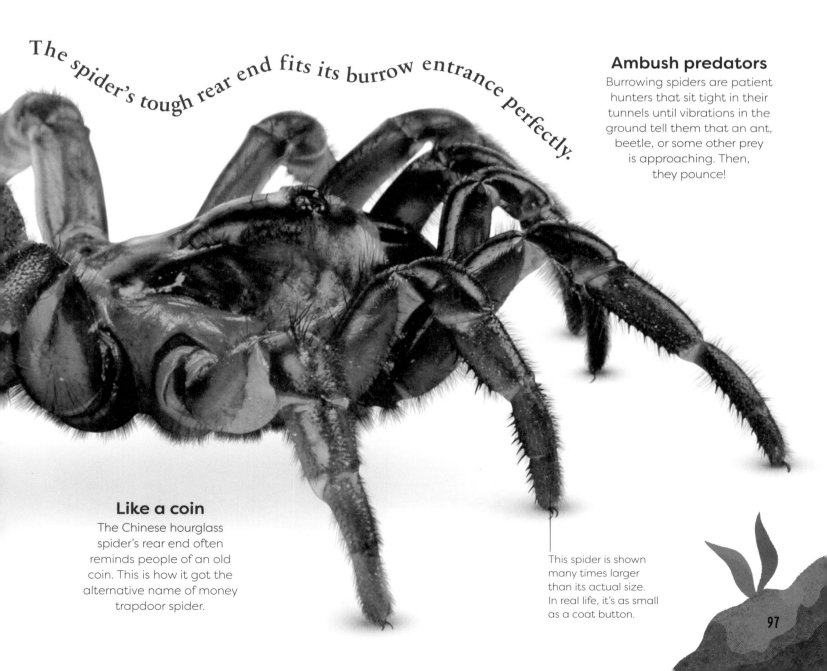

Like a coin

The Chinese hourglass spider's rear end often reminds people of an old coin. This is how it got the alternative name of money trapdoor spider.

This spider is shown many times larger than its actual size. In real life, it's as small as a coat button.

97

Dancing spider

This spider may be tiny, but its dance routine is dazzling.

The peacock spider is smaller than a pea—the photograph to the left shows it much larger than life-size. Yet, it is without doubt one of the greatest dancers in the animal kingdom. It moves incredibly fast and is so athletic it can jump 20 times its body length. This speed and agility come in handy when chasing its insect prey, but also when dancing. Only the male peacock spider dances, though. The goal of the high-energy routine is to persuade a female to mate.

During his dance, a male spider bops up and down, hops from side to side, and circles around the female spider. He lifts up a pair of legs—the third of his four pairs—and waves them like a human dancer with their hands in the air. There is also a fan on his back that he flicks open, like a peacock's tail, to reveal its beautiful shimmering colors. If the female is impressed, she may now mate with him. However, since female spiders often eat males, he has to be careful!

Peacock spider
(*Maratus volans*)
Peacock spiders live in Australia, mostly on the ground. They hide among the undergrowth, so can be hard to spot much of the time.

Dance moves
When the male peacock spider dances around the female, he waves his legs above his head in a particular order. Sometimes he raises a left leg, at other times a right leg, and occasionally both together. The white tufts on the ends of his legs show up like flags.

Different dances

There are more than 100 species of peacock spider, all of which have their own pattern and special dance moves. This coastal peacock spider has a deep blue body.

The third pair of legs is longer than the rest, with fluffy white tips.

This spider's dancing is fast and furious.

A colorful fan is found on the male spider's back.

Sparkle effect

The blue and orange scales on the male spider's body sparkle like glitter when he dances because they catch the sunlight at different angles.

Two massive pairs of eyes face forward for hunting prey.

Dancing

Animals can be great show-offs, but their dancing has a serious purpose. Usually, the goal is to attract a breeding partner—elaborate dances impress mates by showing how fit and healthy the dancers are. However, some dances send warnings or other signals.

Springbok

Springboks often bounce along as if on springs, with all four legs off the ground. The athletic display, called pronking, could be a show of strength or it might be a signal to warn others of danger.

Vogelkop superb bird of paradise

In his courtship dance, the male of this species opens a cape of dark feathers and bounces on the spot to become a twirling black disk on legs. Blue feathers on his head and neck dazzle potential mates.

Striped bark scorpion

Before they mate, some scorpions lock pincers to dance. The male stings the female during their display, although probably not with full-strength venom. This may stop her from attacking him.

Stoat

The stoat, seen here in its white winter coat, sometimes leaps around in a crazy fashion. It could be dancing to hypnotize its prey, so that it can pounce when its confused victims least expect it.

Great blue-spotted mudskipper

These unusual fish have the ability to spend lots of time out of the water on muddy seashores. To impress females, the males open their spotted fins and repeatedly fling themselves into the air.

Blue-footed booby

During the breeding season, the male booby flaunts his colorful webbed feet to attract a mate. He stomps on the ground, lifting one bright blue foot and then the other in a swaying dance.

Cuttlefish skin can produce a flashing light show.

Papuan cuttlefish

Cuttlefish, which are related to octopuses, dance side by side before mating. They swim in tandem and make elaborate shapes in the water as their skin pulses with brilliant colors.

For their final display, the partners hold water weed in their beaks.

Clark's grebe

These lake birds perform complex mating ceremonies, including one in which they run across the water together and another in which they rise up beak to beak and shake their heads.

Fighting back

If a hungry fish takes on the boxer crab, the crab raises its anemones, ready to fight. The sight of the stinging tentacles is usually enough to make the fish back off, but just to make sure, the crab jabs them at its opponent.

Every anemone tentacle is armed with venomous stings.

Urchin defense

The carrier crab walks around hugging a spiny sea urchin with two pairs of legs. The urchin's spines protect the crab from fish and other predators.

This female boxer crab is also defending her sac of eggs.

The anemones this crab holds make it look a little like a cheerleader!

Boxing crab

Thanks to the anemones on its claws, this crab has a punch that stings.

The boxer crab is only little—around the size of a bottle cap—so it is a tempting snack for many other animals on the coral reef. To make up for this, it uses weapons to defend itself. It picks up two anemones and attaches them to its claws as living boxing gloves. The anemones are just a few millimeters long and look like frilly pom-poms, but can pack a painful punch because their tentacles have venom. If the crab hits an attacker, the enemy will be badly stung.

Since the crab has its claws full, they are no longer any use for feeding. Instead, the crab helps itself to bits of food the anemones catch. But how does it find the anemones in the first place? It steals them from other boxer crabs! The crabs often do battle over the anemones and sometimes well-matched fighters end up with one each. When this happens, they simply tear their prize in half and both portions grow back into full-size anemones, one for each claw.

Boxer crab
(Lybia tessellata)

The boxer crab lives on coral reefs in the Pacific Ocean. If its anemones are damaged in a fight, they can regrow.

The crab uses eight legs for walking.

Claws full

The boxer crab's claws have spines to grip the anemones. Since the claws can no longer be used for eating, the crab has to tear up food with its front pair of walking legs.

103

Waving crab

Male fiddler crabs have a gigantic claw that's useless for feeding. Instead, they wave it in the air to impress female crabs or swing it as a weapon to threaten or fight other males who invade their patch of beach. The downside is they have to work twice as hard with their smaller claw to get enough food.

Fish slime factory

Hagfish swamp their enemies with colossal amounts of slime.

When whales and fish die, they sink to the ocean floor. Down here, under immense pressure, their bodies start falling apart. Blood seeps into the dark water, attracting many hungry animals for a feast. One of them is the hagfish, also called the slime eel. It looks like a knee-length pink sock filled with jelly! The hagfish has no eyes, so finds its way by smell, and swims around with its mouth permanently open. As soon as this strange fish locates a carcass, it burrows in headfirst using its strong teeth and tears off chunks of meat.

While the hagfish tucks in, it is at risk of being eaten by a larger fish, but it has an excellent defense. It has more than 100 glands that pump out a material which turns into disgusting slime in under a second. Now, if the attacker tries to swallow the slimy hagfish, the gunge blocks its gills so it can't breathe and the hagfish is quickly spat out. The slime is mostly seawater, but contains threads that rapidly stick together to create a revolting gloopy mixture.

Pacific hagfish
(Eptatretus stoutii)
This hagfish lives in the Pacific Ocean. It is usually found in very deep water, more than 2 miles (3 km) below the surface, where it is always cold and dark.

Tying knots
The hagfish is so soft and flexible, it can tie itself in a knot. This is a handy way to remove the slime from its own skin, once danger has passed. The hagfish slides the knot along its body from head to tail to scrape off the slime.

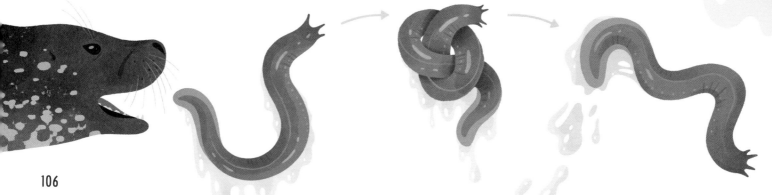

The hagfish is covered in baggy skin. It has no scales or fins.

A hagfish makes bucketfuls of slime in seconds.

Parrotfish sleeping bag

Parrotfish live on coral reefs and every night burp out a sack of slime to sleep in. It probably protects them from bloodsucking parasites.

Jawless fish

Hagfish are an extremely ancient type of fish with no jaws or backbone, although they do have a skull. They have hardly changed in more than 300 million years.

Near the hagfish's mouth there are short tentacles, called barbels, for feeling around.

107

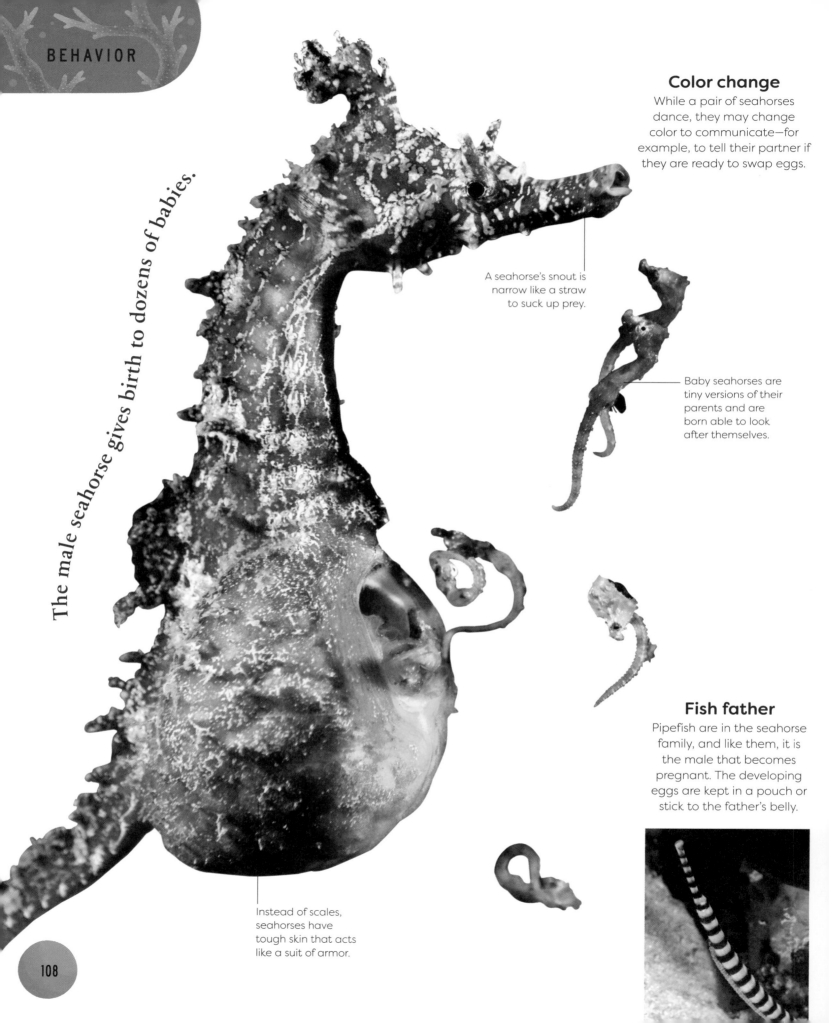

The male seahorse gives birth to dozens of babies.

Color change
While a pair of seahorses dance, they may change color to communicate—for example, to tell their partner if they are ready to swap eggs.

A seahorse's snout is narrow like a straw to suck up prey.

Baby seahorses are tiny versions of their parents and are born able to look after themselves.

Fish father
Pipefish are in the seahorse family, and like them, it is the male that becomes pregnant. The developing eggs are kept in a pouch or stick to the father's belly.

Instead of scales, seahorses have tough skin that acts like a suit of armor.

Pregnant male seahorse

Unusually, it is male seahorses who become pregnant and give birth.

In ancient Greece, seahorses caught in fishing nets were thought to be half-fish and half-horse, but today, we know they are simply unusual-looking fish, not mythical beasts. Unlike most other fish, seahorses swim upright using the fin on their backs. They are weak swimmers, so often coil their long tails around coral or seaweed to stop themselves from drifting away, in much the same way that monkeys grip branches with their tails.

It is normal for male and female fish to lead separate lives—they come together only briefly, to mate, and may not meet again. However, male and female seahorses usually form a strong partnership that lasts the whole breeding season. The partners dance to strengthen their relationship, and when they mate, something extraordinary happens. The female transfers her eggs to the male to look after in a stretchy pouch on his belly. During his pregnancy, the seahorse father sustains his babies just like a mother, and his belly swells massively. He gives birth with powerful twitches of his belly muscles, which push the young out into the water.

Korean seahorse
(*Hippocampus haema*)

Most seahorses are small and stick to shallow water on the coast, including the Korean seahorse, which is barely the size of a crayon.

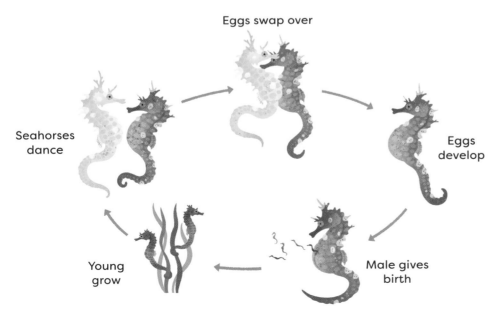

Eggs swap over

Seahorses dance

Eggs develop

Young grow

Male gives birth

Seahorse life cycle

A pair of seahorses greet each other by dancing. They then meet belly to belly so the female can pass her eggs to the male's pouch, where they are fertilized. The male nourishes the babies for two weeks, then gives birth to a new generation of young seahorses.

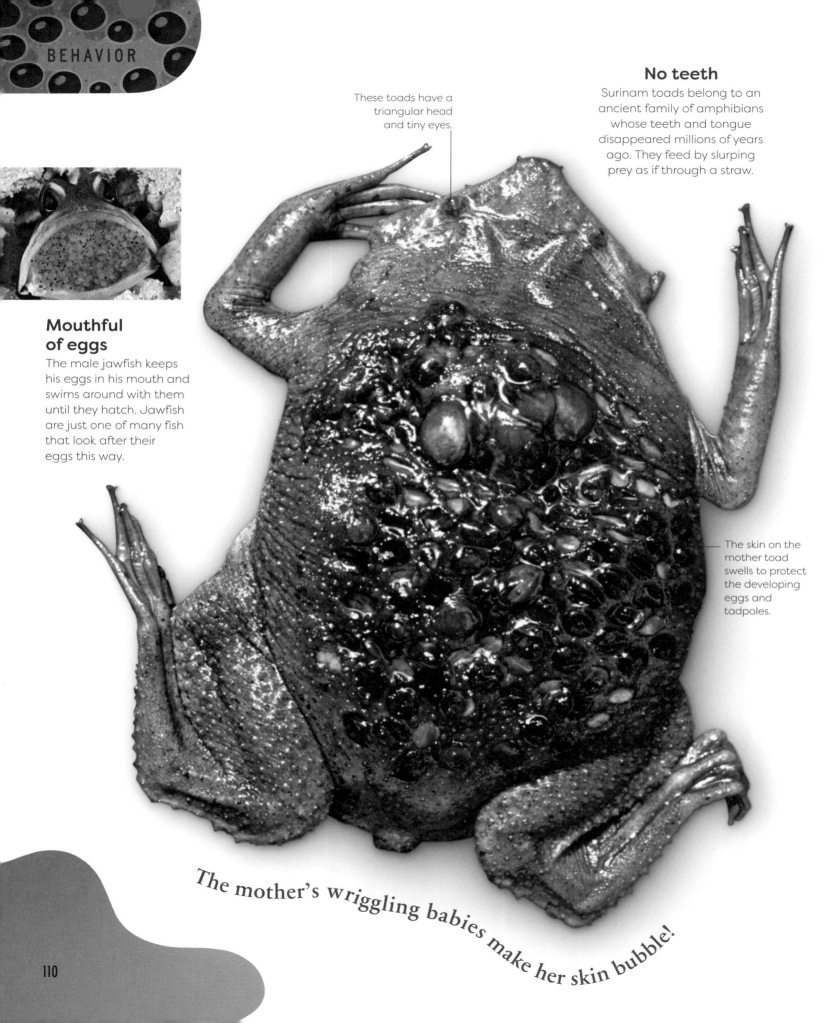

These toads have a triangular head and tiny eyes.

No teeth

Surinam toads belong to an ancient family of amphibians whose teeth and tongue disappeared millions of years ago. They feed by slurping prey as if through a straw.

Mouthful of eggs

The male jawfish keeps his eggs in his mouth and swims around with them until they hatch. Jawfish are just one of many fish that look after their eggs this way.

The skin on the mother toad swells to protect the developing eggs and tadpoles.

The mother's wriggling babies make her skin bubble!

Hatching from skin

Some toads hatch tadpoles out of their own backs.

Toads and frogs have a dangerous start to life. Their eggs and tadpoles make tasty snacks for many other animals, including fish, herons, and even water beetles with deadly jaws. This means female toads and frogs have to release thousands of eggs to make sure enough survive. However, if they guard them, they can lay far fewer. Surinam toads produce only around 100 eggs and go to extraordinary lengths to protect them. When they mate, their fertilized eggs are planted on the female's back, instead of in the water. Her skin then grows over them and swells until it's as bumpy as sheets of plastic packaging bubbles. Each fleshy pocket has an egg inside. When the tadpoles hatch, they continue developing in their strange nurseries. Eventually, the baby toadlets are ready to break free and push their fingers through their mother's bulging skin to make exit holes. If you saw her now, she would have lots of little hands poking out of her back! One by one, the toadlets burst from her body and swim away. The mother toad then sheds her skin, so she is ready to start the process again.

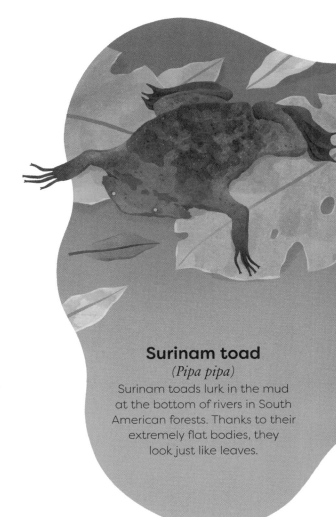

Surinam toad
(Pipa pipa)
Surinam toads lurk in the mud at the bottom of rivers in South American forests. Thanks to their extremely flat bodies, they look just like leaves.

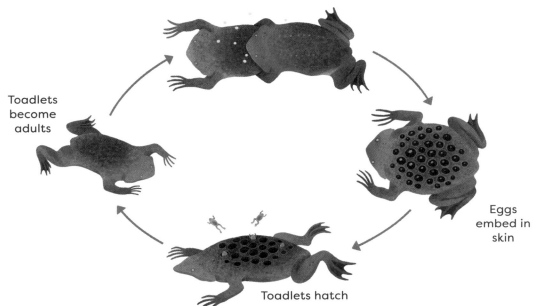

Eggs released

Toadlets become adults

Eggs embed in skin

Toadlets hatch

Toad life cycle

The male and female Surinam toad do somersaults in the water while the female releases her eggs in order to transfer them to her back. The eggs embed in her skin and are safely covered over. The toadlets, which are mini versions of their parents, hatch several months later.

111

Freezing ocean

Because of the salt in the water, the Antarctic Ocean can drop below the freezing point of 32°F (0°C). To survive there, the icefish's blood contains a kind of antifreeze to keep it flowing.

While the frog is frozen, all its body functions are put on hold.

When the frog freezes, its eyes remain open. Their frozen lenses turn white, then clear again as they defrost.

Making antifreeze

The wood frog produces masses of sugar in its liver as antifreeze. The sugar lowers the temperature at which its cells freeze, protecting them in the cold weather.

Frozen frog

During the winter, this frog freezes into a block of ice.

Winters are cold and long in the far north of the planet. The ground stays frozen for seven or eight months, which for most forest frogs would be fatal. Yet, the wood frog of North America can survive these extreme winters. In fall, before the big freeze begins, it fills every cell in its body with sugar. The sugar is a natural antifreeze, so its cells remain unfrozen on the inside, even though ice crystals begin to form on the outside. Incredibly, 75 percent of the frog can turn to ice without doing it any harm. However, in this semi-frozen state, it can't supply its organs with the oxygen and nutrients they need to keep working, so it shuts everything down. Its heart stops beating and its breathing also stops. Barely alive, it rests all winter.

At last, the warmer days of spring bring the frog back to life. First, its heart restarts and its blood begins flowing again, taking oxygen around its body. Then, its muscles start moving and it gulps its first breath in months. When fully defrosted, the frog hops away, as if nothing has happened.

Wood frog
(*Lithobates sylvaticus*)
Wood frogs live in the forests of North America. Those found farthest north, in Alaska and Canada, can cope with the most severe cold and stay frozen the longest.

Winter survival

In October, the wood frog finds a snug spot among dead leaves and nestles down. There, it will remain frozen all winter. On a sunny day in May, the sun's warmth thaws out the frog in as little as 12 hours.

113

Skin-eating amphibian

Baby caecilians feast on their mother's skin.

Mothers in the animal kingdom feed their babies in many ways and may put an astonishing amount of time and energy into this vital task. One of the strangest examples of maternal care is found in caecilians (you say their name "sih-sill-ee-ans.") They look a bit like giant worms, but they have a mouthful of sharp teeth and a backbone, which makes them vertebrates. In fact, they are legless, tail-less amphibians that have taken to an underground life in the soil, hardly ever coming to the surface. Some female caecilians, like other amphibians, reproduce by laying eggs, while others give birth to babies. For certain species of caecilian, though, what happens next is unique. They develop a top layer of fatty skin for their hungry babies to tear off! The skin is obviously tasty, because in the first week alone, the youngsters more than double their body weight. After each feast, they rest for a few days, which gives their mother time to regrow her skin, ready for the next meal.

As an added treat, they lap up a see-through liquid that she releases from her bottom!

Grooves in the animal's skin stretch and squeeze like an accordion to move it through the soil.

Ringed caecilian
(*Siphonops annulatus*)
This unusual amphibian burrows in the soil throughout much of South America. It is named for the white rings around its body and grows up to 16 in (40 cm) long.

Special skin

The skin of the mother ringed caecilian swells up and fills with fat to nourish her babies. She lies still to let them tuck in, using their three rows of sharp teeth. It takes just seven minutes or so for the young to remove all of the extra skin.

Mom on the menu

The female black lace-weaver spider is one of the most devoted mothers. She feeds her babies with her own body—the spiderlings can suck it dry within hours.

Venomous bite

Scientists in Brazil have discovered caecilians with venom glands in their mouths, perhaps for defense. Many amphibians have poisonous skin, but these are the world's only venomous ones.

Baby caecilians eagerly tear strips off their mother.

Ringed caecilians have tiny eyes covered in skin, leaving them sightless. They find earthworm prey by smell.

Like other amphibians, a caecilian can breathe through its thin, moist skin as well as its lungs.

Hot-footed hopper

During the day, desert sand heats up even faster
than the air and may hit 160°F (70°C)—hot enough
to fry an egg. This is a blistering problem for any
animal touching it. The shovel-snouted lizard of
southern Africa's Namib Desert keeps its feet cool
by lifting them up two at a time, as if dancing.

Barred grass snake
(Natrix helvetica)
A better name for this European snake would be "water snake," because it usually lives near ponds and marshy places and likes to swim.

Snake playing dead

The grass snake pretends to be dead to confuse its enemies.

Many people tend to assume that all snakes are venomous, but actually, most are not. For every species of snake in the world with venom, there are at least four others without it. You might think that this would leave nonvenomous snakes unable to defend themselves from predators—of which there are many, including other snakes. However, while these snakes may not be toxic, they know a few tricks to keep themselves safe. Often their first move is to hiss loudly and rear up to frighten an enemy. They also produce a disgusting smell that reeks of poop or rotten eggs.

If that fails, some snakes, such as grass snakes in Europe and hognose snakes in North America, try something more dramatic. They stop moving and act dead. The sudden change startles the predator, who was expecting to kill a live animal, not eat a "dead" one. The trick is so successful that even a few venomous snakes, including cobras, have learned to do it as well! It allows them to save their precious venom for hunting.

Defense mechanism

When a predator, such as a domestic cat, paws at a grass snake, the snake flips onto its back and opens its mouth so its tongue hangs out. The cat stops what it's doing, which gives the "dead" snake its chance. It springs back to life and escapes.

The snake's acting is very convincing.

Apparent death

The Virginia opossum, which lives in North America, is one of the few mammals that plays dead. When in danger, it drops to the ground and lets its mouth loll open.

The tongue hangs out of the open jaws and stops moving.

Awful smell

If they are in trouble, snakes can release a thick, gooey, foul-smelling liquid from a pair of glands near their tails.

The snake twists around to expose the scales on its belly.

119

The horns on the frill have a bony center, like the horns of cattle, sheep, and goats.

Bone breaker
The hairy frog can break its own toe bones, which burst out of its skin like spikes to give its enemies a fright. No wonder its other name is "horror frog."

The lizard squirts blood up to 3 ft (1 m) away.

Some scales are pointed to form sharp spines.

Blood stains the lizard's face after dealing with an enemy.

Water collector
Water is hard to find in the desert. Droplets collect on the scales on this lizard's back, then drip into gaps between its other scales and flow toward its mouth.

Blood-squirting lizard

When under attack, the horned lizard shoots blood from its eyes.

The horned lizard is well camouflaged in its desert home, but if a predator spots one and tries to attack, it is likely to regret it. For a start, the lizard has heavy-duty armor. Its body is covered in spines, and horns create a spiked frill around its head. It looks a bit like a miniature version of the dinosaur Triceratops. Most predators move on when they see how well protected the lizard is, but if they keep coming, it does something amazing. It shoots blood at them!

Here's how it works. Muscles squeeze the veins around the lizard's eyes. This traps blood under the eyes and the skin there starts to bulge. As the lizard squeezes even harder, the skin splits, and blood gushes from the corner of both eye sockets. The lizard's shocked enemy is soaked and usually runs away. The lizard has won. All this takes just a few moments, but if it has to, the lizard can shoot blood several times. The defense works best against coyotes and domestic dogs, which seem to find the lizard blood particularly revolting.

Three defenses

The horned lizard's horns and spines are its first defense when attacked. Its next tactic is to puff up, so it appears larger and the spines stick out. If that does not put the predator off, the lizard's final move is to squirt jets of blood.

Regal horned lizard
(Phrynosoma solare)
Horned lizards live in deserts in Mexico and the Southern US. They prey mainly on ants, which they lick up with their powerful tongues.

Regal horned lizard

Coyote

121

Colorful crest

Male and female hoopoes raise their huge crest feathers when displaying. Considered a holy bird in ancient Egypt, they were often painted on tomb walls.

Male and female

With their crest hidden, female and male royal flycatchers look much the same and it's hard to tell them apart. But what a difference when they flick their crests open! The female's crest is yellow, but the male's crest is red.

Female

Male

The head feathers fan out like a peacock's tail.

The crest feathers have purple spots and bluish tips.

Displaying bird

Royal flycatchers are easy to miss— until they reveal their "crown."

Split ends

The longest feathers in a royal flycatcher's crest are frayed at the tip, which gives it a fringed edge.

The tropical forests of South America are home to more bird species than anywhere else on Earth. Here, you will find rainbow-colored parrots that caw loudly, huge harpy eagles that hunt monkeys, and hummingbirds that can fly backward and loop through the air. If you're lucky, you may also find royal flycatchers. Small and brown in appearance, and quiet in their rare calls to each other, these birds keep a low profile in the forest. However, they can put on an extraordinary display.

On top of both the male and female's head is a large crest that they can raise to form a "crown," giving them their name. The flycatchers also sway from side to side to make their crest feathers quiver, and open and close their bills to show off the bright orange skin inside their mouths. Sometimes, male birds will perform this dance to try to impress a female. At other times, male and female pairs will perform the display together, to warn other intruding flycatchers away from their patch of forest or to confuse a predator.

Stiff hairs protect the bird's eyes from its insect prey, such as dragonflies and grasshoppers.

Amazonian royal flycatcher

(Onychorhynchus coronatus)

These birds live in South America's vast Amazon rain forest. They make sock-shaped nests, which hang from branches over rivers as protection against predators.

123

African death's-head hawkmoth

This moth from Africa and Europe is named after the skull-like pattern behind its head. Part of its warning display is almost unique among insects—if something threatens it, it squeaks like a mouse!

Bright yellow underwings can be flashed to startle a predator.

The bird's mouth is bright orange inside, which adds to the effect.

Tawny frogmouth

Frogmouths open their beaks enormously wide to catch prey, and they use the same trick to scare enemies such as snakes and birds of prey. Their huge staring eyes make the display even more alarming.

Threat displays

The natural world is full of predators—and that means animals have to defend themselves. They can stay safe with weapons, armor, camouflage, poison, or stings... but what if they don't have any of these? Another clever way to deal with attackers is to spring a surprise that bamboozles or frightens them.

Malaysian dead leaf mantis

When in danger, this insect raises its claws and wings to reveal a startling pattern underneath. Two spots that look a lot like eyes make the mantis appear to be a much larger animal.

Eastern spotted skunk

Skunks are fairly small, so predators might think they're an easy target, but to make up for their size, they spray a foul liquid from glands near their bottoms. However, they do a handstand first as a warning.

Frill-necked lizard

This Australian lizard can unfold the skin around its neck to create a large "umbrella," while also hissing and cracking its tail like a whip. The display makes predators think twice, giving the lizard time to escape.

Sarcastic fringehead

These fish have a bizarre threat display that they use on each other. When two of them argue over food, they open their jaws wider than their own heads. The fish with the biggest mouth wins!

Peacock butterfly

If a hungry bird approaches this butterfly, it suddenly flicks its wings open to display four huge, colorful spots that look like eyes. The surprise is often enough to scare the attacker away.

Long-eared owl

Baby birds are vulnerable to predators when their parents are away from the nest. Young long-eared owls fluff up their feathers and stretch their wings to look as big as they can.

Pom-pom caterpillar

Should anything touch the caterpillar of the angled sunbeam butterfly, it does something very surprising. It shoots out a pair of pom-poms from tubes on its rear end and twirls them rapidly. The effect is so scary, shocked predators don't hang around. Only the caterpillar has this ability—it loses its pom-poms when it becomes a butterfly.

Alarm service

When oxpeckers see a predator, they chatter in alarm. Rhinos have learned to recognize these alarm calls, so the birds on their backs help alert them to danger.

Finch attack

The vampire finch pecks seabirds to make them bleed and then laps up the blood with its tongue. It lives on the Galápagos Islands.

The bill is smooth and flat, which helps it slide under hair easily.

The bird's long toes and claws give it a firm grip.

The oxpecker's diet includes ear wax and dandruff!

Blood-sipping bird

Like a vampire, the oxpecker perches on other animals to sip their blood.

Africa's giraffes often have birds riding on them. So do zebras, antelopes, buffaloes, and rhinos. Herds of cows do, too. These feathered passengers are oxpeckers. The animals on whose backs the birds are perched do not seem to mind them. In return for their free ride, the oxpeckers offer a sort of cleaning service. Using their scissor-shaped bills, they expertly search their host's fur for small pests, including ticks, lice, fleas, and maggots—the larvae of flies. Any they find are quickly removed and swallowed. It must not hurt, because the hosts will allow the oxpeckers to nibble around their eyes and mouth and reach right inside their ears!

However, there is another side to the relationship between the oxpeckers and their hosts. These birds are vampires as well. They peck at wounds to make the blood flow. It gives them a nutritious meal, but may weaken the host animals they feed from. Not all animals tolerate oxpeckers—they are rarely seen on elephants, for example. Before the birds can start to feed, the elephants shoo them away with their trunks and huge, flapping ears.

Red-billed oxpecker
(*Buphagus erythrorynchus*)
Oxpeckers, including the red-billed oxpecker, are found across Africa's grassy plains wherever there are wild mammals or herds of cattle to feed from. They are about the size of starlings.

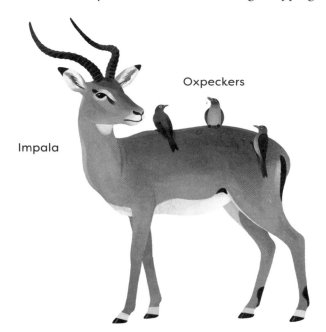

Oxpeckers

Impala

Bird parasites

Oxpeckers search a host's fur for small prey, but also keep an eye out for the chance of a meal of blood. Their bills are not strong enough to cut into the host's skin, but if they discover a fresh wound, they enlarge it to sip the blood.

129

The red balloon inflates to the size of a soccer ball.

Diving deep

Hooded seals can hold their breath for more than 30 minutes during dives up to half a mile (1 km) below the surface in search of fish.

The head balloon reaches from the seal's mouth to just behind its eyes.

Deflated nose

In its normal position with no air in it, the bright nose balloon is hidden inside the seal's left nostril.

Inflating seal

The male hooded seal can blow up two huge balloons on its head and nose.

Finding a breeding partner is one of the most important things many animals will ever have to do. Male seals often fight to show who is fittest and to attract females, but male hooded seals do something no other seal can. Instead of taking part in battles, they blow up a pair of enormous balloons on their heads to show off! One is black, the other bright red. With their two balloons inflated, the seals look utterly ridiculous to us, and yet this weird display does the trick. The seal with the biggest and best balloons wins the contest, and is able to breed.

The balloons are connected to the male seal's nose. To inflate the black balloon, he closes both nostrils and fills it with air until it expands into a huge hood on top of his head. To inflate the red balloon, he closes his right nostril and blows hard down the left one to push it out of his nose. Male hooded seals develop these bizarre balloons at around six years old, but at first they are quite small. Older males look far more impressive.

Hooded seal
(Cystophora cristata)
Hooded seals spend all year in the icy waters of the Arctic Ocean, but haul themselves onto floating sea ice to rest, find mates, and have their pups.

Balloon contest

When two male hooded seals want to impress the same female, the rivals face each other and inflate their balloons. These make pinging and popping sounds as the seals shake their heads. The noisiest, most spectacular male is the victor, while the disappointed loser swims off.

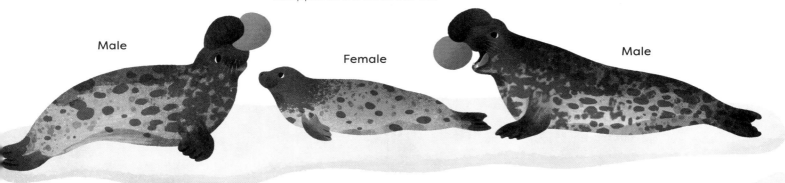

Male

Female

Male

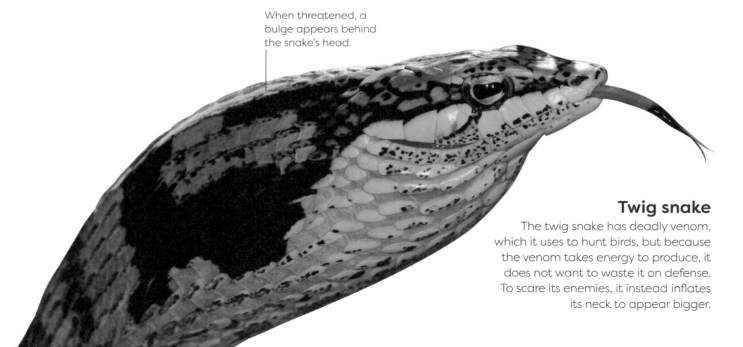

The spines only stick out when the fish inflates itself.

Long-spine porcupine fish

If in danger, a porcupine fish gulps water into its stretchy stomach. Because its skin is also stretchy, and it has fewer ribs than other fish, it quickly balloons to twice its normal size.

When threatened, a bulge appears behind the snake's head.

Twig snake

The twig snake has deadly venom, which it uses to hunt birds, but because the venom takes energy to produce, it does not want to waste it on defense. To scare its enemies, it instead inflates its neck to appear bigger.

Inflating animals

Blowing yourself up like a balloon is a clever trick many animals have mastered. Most do it by taking in huge amounts of air, but fish do it by swallowing water. Believe it or not, the sudden transformation is a brilliant way to scare off enemies, create powerful sounds, and impress a partner!

Magnificent frigate bird

To attract a mate, the male frigate bird pumps up a bag of red skin on his throat until it's the size of a melon. For added effect, he rattles his bill on it like a drum.

Painted reed frog

Male frogs have a sac on their throats that can inflate when they call. Air rushes backward and forward between their lungs and this sac to create a loud sound.

Guineafowl puffer fish

Within seconds, a puffer fish can gulp enough water to make it very difficult for a predator to swallow. When danger has passed, it deflates by forcing the water back out.

Siamang

Every morning, these apes sing a deafening duet to defend their patch of forest. A pouch on their throats inflates like a balloon to make their screams even louder.

Greater sage grouse

The male sage grouse can fill a pair of sacs on his chest with air. They help him produce an extraordinary variety of coos, pops, huffs, and whistles during his courtship display.

American toad

When this toad meets a predator, it lifts its body as high as it can and sucks in air to puff itself up. The toad looks bigger than it really is, so the enemy is much less likely to attack.

Forward-facing eyes help the lemur to judge its leaps perfectly.

When jumping, the lemur lifts its arms to shoulder height.

Swimming sloth

Sloths live in trees and are built for climbing, so—like sifakas—they can't walk on the ground. However, the pygmy three-toed sloth swims well and paddles around in search of a mate.

The lemur flies up to 16 ft (5 m) in a single bound.

The lemur's muscular legs act as powerful springs.

Balancing act

The lemur's long, thick tail provides balance as it leaps from tree to tree or across the ground.

Leaping lemur

This amazing acrobat bounces over the ground as if it's skipping.

On a forest trail, a handsome animal with snow-white fur jumps down from a tree and bounds across the red earth. It moves like a ballet dancer, with elegant footwork and outstretched arms. Every leap sends it sailing through the air. Soon it jumps up into another tree and is gone. This is Verreaux's sifaka (you say its name "veh-rows sah-fah-ka.") It is a type of lemur, and like all lemurs, lives only on the island of Madagascar. The leaping is a clever way of crossing open areas in its forest home. This lemur is adapted for life in the trees and it can't scurry on all-fours because its arms are shorter than its legs. It can't walk upright either, because moving one leg after the other, like we do, is too difficult. So it leaps.

Walking on two legs is one of the things that sets humans apart from animals. Chimpanzees, gorillas, orangutans, and some monkeys do it some of the time, but it takes a lot of effort. Humans find it easy, as the curves in our spine keep our body steady when we are upright.

Verreaux's sifaka
(Propithecus verreauxi)
Verreaux's sifaka is one of the rarest lemurs in Madagascar. It lives in dry forests, where there are strange, spiny trees that look like cacti.

Sideways leap
When on the ground, the lemur seems to skip along with sideways leaps. It crosses its feet in midair and moves its arms up and down for balance, then lands on one leg, ready to push off again.

Larva-fishing lemur

The aye-aye catches insect larvae with its incredibly long middle finger.

When night falls, the mysterious aye-aye leaves its leafy nest to explore the forest. It has big eyes like a cat, leathery ears like a bat, and a bushy tail like a fox. Its sharp front teeth grow nonstop like a rodent's, and the middle finger on its hands is bony, bendy, and twice as long as all the others. You can see why this curious animal confused the scientists who first saw it! In the end, they figured out it is a primate and belongs to the lemur family.

As the aye-aye moves through the trees, it taps the branches repeatedly with its long middle finger. Tap, tap, tap it goes. It listens hard while it does this because a change in the sound shows there is a tunnel under the bark, perhaps with a beetle larva inside. Thanks to its long, hooklike finger, the aye-aye is the only animal in the forest able to reach this juicy meal. Scientists have noticed the aye-aye uses its special finger for something else, too. Picking its nose!

Aye-aye
(Daubentonia madagascariensis)
Like other lemurs, the aye-aye is unique to the island of Madagascar. It is endangered because of hunting and because the forests where it lives are being cut down.

Larva fishing
An aye-aye raps on a tree trunk with its ear pressed to the bark. When it hears a change in pitch, it knows it has found a larva tunnel. It makes a hole in the bark with its front teeth, then pushes in its middle finger to fish out the insect.

The aye-aye taps trees much like a woodpecker.

The huge ears are cup-shaped to capture sound.

Termite fishing

Some chimpanzees use sticks as tools to fish termites out of their nest. They learn by watching older chimps.

Night vision

Like many other nocturnal mammals, the aye-aye has a reflective layer at the back of its eyes to help it see in low light.

The middle finger can swivel in every direction, as our shoulders do.

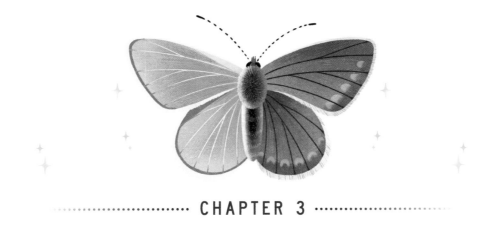

CHAPTER 3

Phenomena

Remarkable natural events,
or phenomena, occur all around the world.
They include weird weather, the creation of strange
natural patterns or structures, and the appearance
of plants and animals that look completely different
than usual. However, they are not something
we see every day. We only come across them
in certain places and only when the conditions
are just right. Many phenomena are
caused by random chance!

Fused flower

A few plants do not grow in the usual way and end up massively distorted.

Every now and then, gardeners and farmers come across weird plants that look different from all the others. They seem to have been stretched and pulled out of shape by a powerful yet mysterious force. Sometimes, their stems are much flatter and wider. On other occasions, several flowers appear to have joined together to form a huge flower head. Fruits may be affected, too, leaving them with bizarre bulges and swellings.

What is going on? The unusual plants have a rare condition called fasciation (you say it "fash-ee-ay-shun.") This changes how they grow and the results can be dramatic. Scientists have several theories to explain why these plants grow this way. It could be down to chemical changes that alter their growth pattern. Or it might be caused by a virus, bacteria, or fungus that has invaded the plants' tissues. Another possibility is that while growing, the plants were damaged—for example, by a severe frost in winter. The changes are not always a problem—some gardeners actually like them and take cuttings from the affected plants to try to produce more.

The yellow area in the middle of the daisy is made up of many separate tiny flowers. There are far more of them than usual.

Common daisy
(*Bellis perennis*)
Many lawns and grassy fields are covered in daisies, but only a few will develop fasciated flowers, which means they are a very rare find!

The fasciated daisy head is the size of several ordinary daisies' heads.

Unusual growth

Fasciation happens when there is a change to a plant's growing tip, called the meristem, found at the very end of a plant's stems. This causes them to grow unusually long and flat. It also alters the overall shape of flowers or fruits that grow from them.

Regular meristem

Lengthened meristem

This fasciated daisy has lots and lots of white petal-like flowers around its edge.

Pruning plants

There is a simple method of dealing with plant fasciation. You simply cut away, or prune, the affected part of the plant. Most causes of fasciation aren't inherited, so don't reoccur.

Fasciation in fruits

Fasciation produces strange growths in fruits such as apples and strawberries. Often there appears to be two, three, or more fruits all growing fused together.

141

Spotted plains

Strange disks of bare red earth, known as "fairy circles," dot the dry plains of southwestern Africa. Most are around the size of a backyard trampoline, and together they make spotted patterns that stretch for many miles. No one is sure what makes them—it might be antlike termites nibbling away all the grass above their underground nests.

Two-tone lobster

Occasionally, Atlantic lobsters have a blue female side and a male orange side. Two-tone lobsters are incredible, but so rare that very few people ever get to see one.

The dual-sex butterfly is divided neatly down the middle.

The female left side has brown wings with orange spots.

Tricky name

The scientific name for this condition is a bit of a mouthful: bilateral gynandromorphism (you say it "bi-lat-er-al gine-an-dro-morf-izm"). Animals with the condition are called gynandromorphs.

The butterfly's right side is male and has blue wings.

144

Male and female

Some animals are split down the middle, with one half male and the other female.

Butterflies, like most insects, are beautifully symmetrical. Each side is a mirror image of the other. Very rarely, however, there is an error early in their development. The result is a butterfly with two sexes, one on each side of its body! It is as if a male and a female butterfly have been divided and the opposite halves stuck back together again. Sometimes, the left half is male and the right half female, and sometimes it's the other way around. With their mismatched wings, these dual-sex butterflies are spectacular, but extremely unusual.

On average, out of every 10,000 butterflies, just one is dual-sex. The condition occurs in other insects, too, and in a few of them, such as earwigs, it can actually be quite common. There are also half-male, half-female spiders, lobsters, crabs, and birds—all of which look extraordinary. In North America, for example, a handful of people have seen dual-sex cardinals on their garden bird feeders. These birds are cherry-red on their male side and grayish-brown on their female side!

Common blue butterfly
(Polyommatus icarus)
These pretty butterflies flit through many flowery places in Asia and Europe. Males are pale blue, while females are the color of milk chocolate with a border of orange spots.

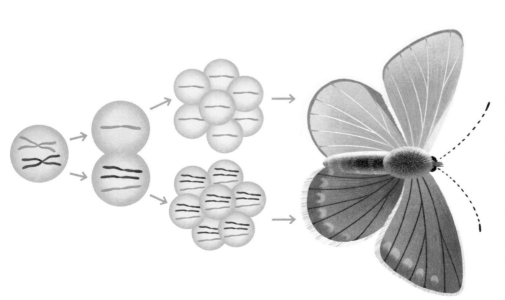

Cell division error
Cells contain structures called chromosomes and some of these determine an animal's sex. Usually, when an embryo starts to develop, the first cell divides to produce two male cells or two female cells. If there is an error, one male and one female cell can be created instead, and as the cells continue to divide, it creates a dual-sex butterfly.

145

Magnetic termite mound

These termite nests always line up in a north-south direction.

We are living on a gigantic magnet. Deep inside the Earth, liquid iron churns like cement in a cement mixer. The currents in the hot, molten metal combined with the Earth's spin make the iron swirl around. This motion creates the magnetic field that surrounds the planet. Although the field is invisible, it can be felt by many animals, such as sea turtles, sharks, lobsters, and birds, as well as insects.

In Australia, insects called termites use their magnetic sense to build their nests. They make flattened mounds of sun-baked soil, and the thin edge always points north-south. So, without fail, the mounds line up. But why? It stops the mounds from overheating. During the hottest part of the day, only the thin edge faces north into the fierce sun. The rest of the mound is in the shade, so stays at a more comfortable temperature for the termites. Grassy plains can be filled with hundreds of these termite mounds, all arranged in a neat grid—they look like sculptures made by humans, but the termites that built them are only about 0.02 in (5 mm) long.

Magnetic termite
(Amitermes meridionalis)
The world has several thousand kinds of termite, but just two are known to build magnetic mounds, including the magnetic termite. Both types live in the grassy plains of northern Australia.

Temperature control

A mound's position and shape keep it at a steady temperature. The east side faces the sun in the morning and the west side faces it in the afternoon. They are wide and flat because the sun is not as warm at these times of day. The north side, which faces the hot noon sun, is thinner, to avoid its scorching rays.

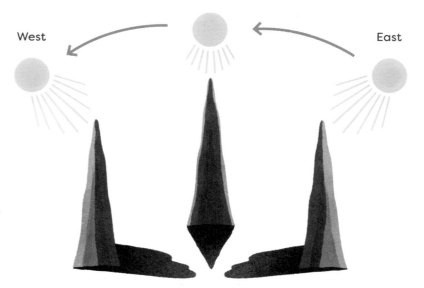

West   East

Huge home

Each mound can be up to 13 ft (4 m) tall. It is home to a termite colony, including thousands of workers that gather food, soldier termites that defend the nest, and a single queen.

The thick walls are made of soil glued together with termite spit and poop.

Returning home

Sea turtles sense the Earth's magnetic field as they swim across the ocean. They use it to find their way back to the same beach where they hatched years earlier.

Inside the mound it is a constant 86°F (30°C).

The termites eat dead grass and store vast amounts of it in their mound.

Shared webs

In spring, enormous ghostly webs appear, which may be large enough to cover entire trees and hedges in white silk. They don't belong to spiders but to swarms of moth caterpillars. Safe from predators, the thousands of hungry caterpillars living inside can strip every leaf to the stem. The huge webs break up by the time the caterpillars change into moths.

149

Male to female

Clown fish live in groups led by a large female and her male partner. When the ruling female dies, the male changes sex to take her place.

These fish make the dramatic switch in just 10 days.

Females and some males are mainly yellow. They can't be told apart.

Adult supermales have a blue head that sparkles in the sunlight.

Cleaning service

Blue-headed wrasse love to feed on the parasites and dead scales of other fish. They advertise their helpful service by swimming a sort of jerky dance to attract fish that want to be cleaned.

Changing sex

Some fish can switch sex midway through their life.

Earth's tropical coral reefs are dazzling habitats, home to glittering schools of rainbow-colored fish. You will find more kinds of fish around reefs than in any other part of the sea and around a quarter of them can change their sex. They start out as male or female, then swap. One of these is the blue-headed wrasse, which scientists have studied in great detail. Some wrasse hatch from eggs as male fish and stay male all their lives. Others hatch female and remain female. However, a small number of females undergo a change to become adult "supermales." They now rule the roost and defend a territory on the seabed. The trigger is usually the death of an existing supermale, which creates a vacancy that needs to be filled.

Most sex-changing fish, like the blue-headed wrasse, go from female to male. Only a few, such as clown fish, start off male and become female. In most cases, the sex change is permanent, but parrotfish change back and forth many times. The tiny chalk bass from the Caribbean switches sex up to 20 times a day!

Blue-headed wrasse
(Thalassoma bifasciatum)
Schools of these little fish dart through coral reefs and seagrass meadows in the Atlantic Ocean. They are named after the bright colors of the adult supermales.

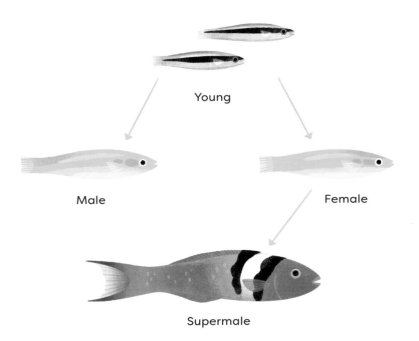

Young

Male

Female

Supermale

Spectacular change
Young blue-headed wrasse have black and white stripes. Over time, the juvenile fish lose their stripes and develop yellowish bodies, although at this stage it's still not possible to tell which sex they are. However, a handful of them—always females—will eventually turn into colorful adult supermales.

Inheriting albinism

Albinism is caused by a recessive gene. This means it is dominated by the gene for green. Most genes are inherited in pairs, and if a baby alligator inherits one green gene and one albino gene, the effects of the albino gene are hidden. If it inherits two copies of the albino gene—one from each parent—it will have albinism.

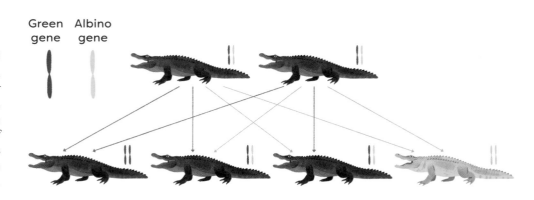

Green gene | Albino gene

This albino alligator is almost pure white.

Alligator claws are usually dark, but they are pale in albino animals.

Famous whale

Some albino animals have become famous. An albino male humpback whale nicknamed "Migaloo," which was first spotted in 1991 off the coast of Australia, became a global celebrity.

Albinism

A rare genetic change gives albino animals a pale appearance.

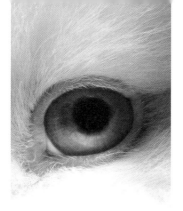

Red eyes
Albino animals often seem to have pink or red eyes. Since there is little or no pigment in the iris and other parts of the eye, the red blood inside shows through.

The scales are white, instead of the typical grayish-green.

Animals inherit many characteristics from their parents. These features are passed on by genes, which are made up of the substance DNA. You can think of genes as sets of instructions to build a baby animal as it develops. Random changes, known as mutations, can take place in the DNA, some of which produce albinism. This condition causes an animal to make little or none of a dark pigment called melanin, which results in the animal's skin, fur, scales, feathers, or shell being pale or white. There are even albino plants, which lack the green pigment chlorophyll.

Albino animals often have health problems—for example, their pale skin is vulnerable to sunburn. They also stand out from the crowd, which makes it easier for predators to target them, so they usually don't survive long. Only a few breed and pass their genes on to the next generation, which makes albino animals even scarcer. People can also have albinism, whatever their race or skin color, but it is rare. On average, one in every 10,000–20,000 people worldwide is thought to have albinism.

American alligator
(Alligator mississippiensis)
These alligators live in the swamps and lakes of the southeastern US and are green in color. Wild albino alligators are very rare, although there are a few in zoos.

153

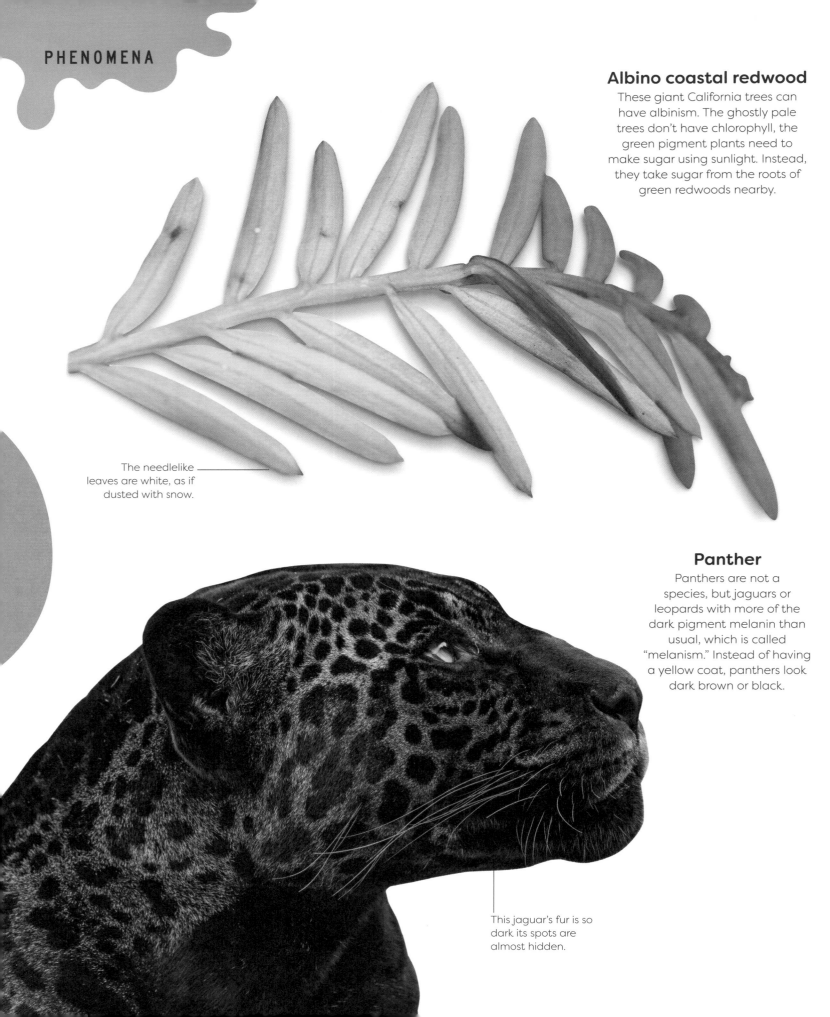

Albino coastal redwood

These giant California trees can have albinism. The ghostly pale trees don't have chlorophyll, the green pigment plants need to make sugar using sunlight. Instead, they take sugar from the roots of green redwoods nearby.

The needlelike leaves are white, as if dusted with snow.

Panther

Panthers are not a species, but jaguars or leopards with more of the dark pigment melanin than usual, which is called "melanism." Instead of having a yellow coat, panthers look dark brown or black.

This jaguar's fur is so dark its spots are almost hidden.

Different colors

Occasionally, we see animals or plants that look different from the rest. Their unique colors are caused by having more or less of different pigments. This can be due to a particular gene they have inherited or a change in their pigment cells.

Albino cactus seedling

Albinism occurs in plants as well as animals. It is caused by lack of pigment, but without the pigment chlorophyll, albino plants can't make their own food using sunlight, so usually die as seedlings.

Yellow northern cardinal

Male northern cardinals are usually bright red, but sometimes people see one that is orange or yellow. Their feathers have more yellow pigment and less red pigment. Birds get red and yellow pigments from their food.

Point coloration rabbit

A few breeds of pets, including domestic rabbits, have a gene that produces dark pigment only in cooler parts of the body. This can result in darker fur at certain "points," such as the ears, nose, and paws.

Yellow Burmese python

These large snakes have a pale form with golden, creamy, or peachy skin. It is caused by them not having the dark pigment melanin, but they still produce a yellow pigment called xanthin.

Red grasshopper

Grasshoppers can turn bright pink, which is known as "erythrism." This is caused by a change in their genes that makes the insects produce more red pigment than they usually would.

Pale blackbird

European blackbirds, like many other birds, can have plumage that is all or partly white. They lack any pigment in the affected areas and we say they have "leucism." Unlike animals with albinism, they do not have red eyes.

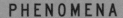

Hybrid animal

When different species mate, they produce distinct-looking young called hybrids.

Birdwatchers sometimes spot strange ducks that don't match any of the pictures in identification guides. The puzzling ducks have a mixture of features because they are hybrids, created when two different species of duck mated and produced young. The hybrids inherit physical and behavioral characteristics from each species and end up as a combination of both. Many animals are able to produce hybrids, but they must usually belong to the same genus, or group, of species. For example, lions and tigers can breed together since they are both big cats, whereas lions and wolves cannot.

Hybrids occur naturally when related species share the same habitat. In parts of North America, male polar bears occasionally wander inland into areas used by female grizzly bears. If they mate, their cubs often have a white coat with brown legs. When people breed hybrids in captivity, it is known as crossbreeding or crossing. A mule is born when a male donkey is crossed with a female horse. Mules have been bred for thousands of years because they are strong and confident over rocky ground, which makes them useful for carrying goods.

Liger
(Panthera leo x Panthera tigris)
A liger is a hybrid cat with a male lion and female tiger as parents. Ligers only exist in captivity because wild lions and tigers rarely meet in the wild.

Hybrid crosses
When a male lion is crossed with a female tiger, the result is a hybrid cat called a liger. However, if a male tiger is crossed with a female lion, the hybrid they produce looks very different and is known as a tigon. Like many hybrids, ligers and tigons often suffer from poor health.

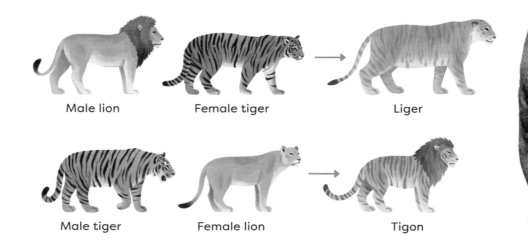

Male lion   Female tiger   Liger

Male tiger   Female lion   Tigon

Having young

Some hybrid animals are fertile, meaning they can mate and have young of their own. Others are always infertile and unable to breed.

Ligers have a mixture of both lion and tiger features.

This hybrid cat has the mane and fur color of a lion but the stripes of a tiger.

Striped horse

If a male zebra and female horse breed, they produce a zorse. This hybrid usually has faint zebralike stripes, but keeps some horselike coloration, too.

Ligers can be larger than the largest lion or tiger. This makes them the biggest cats on Earth.

157

Hair ice is a mass of
separate strands.

Hair ice fungus

This fungus eats dead wood. It also helps hair ice form and keep its shape. When water in the wood freezes, the fungus enables it to be slowly squeezed out of tiny holes into thin strands.

Hair ice grows overnight, but soon melts in the morning sun.

The ice has a wonderful gleam to it, like pearl.

Thin strands

The strands in hair ice are made from many individual ice crystals joined together. Each strand is no more than 0.0008 in (0.02 mm) thick—that's thinner than the average human hair.

158

Hair ice

This fluffy ice is a winter wonder—and very rare.

On a crisp winter morning, when the ground is frozen and your breath forms misty clouds in the frosty air, you might be in for a treat. A woodland walk in these conditions is your best chance of finding hair ice, a mysterious substance like white cotton candy or glossy white hair. It is no ordinary ice. Tufts of it sprout from logs and fallen branches lying on the ground, and if you peer closer, you will notice the ice is made of delicate wispy strands. These give it a strange texture—it's more like fabric than the cubes of ice or snow you might be more familiar with.

Hair ice, which is also known as "frost beard," only occurs in certain situations. The wood on which it grows must be rotting, not have any bark, and contain a particular kind of fungus. In addition, the wood needs to be wet and warmer than the freezing air. Everything has to be just right. You need to get up early, too, because this winter marvel often melts in the first rays of sunshine.

Hair ice
Most reports of hair ice come from damp winter woods in northern parts of the world, including Asia, Europe, and North America. Sometimes, it occurs in exactly the same place year after year.

Ice crystals

Crystals of ice start to appear when water droplets freeze, either high in the cold sky or on freezing surfaces. As more droplets freeze onto the growing crystals, they develop a huge variety of beautiful shapes. Many have six sides, and the most complex crystals, with a branching pattern, are called snowflakes.

Plates

Needles

Columns

Snowflakes

Icy plates

When a river or polar sea chills to freezing point, slushy ice starts to form on the surface. Currents in the water may then shape the ice into beautiful floating disks. These ice pancakes can be as large as truck tires and up to 4 in (10 cm) thick, with crumpled edges like the crust on a pie.

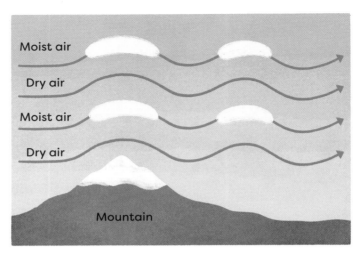

Lenticular cloud formation

As wind blows up and over mountains, the fast-moving air can be pushed into a series of invisible waves. If the waves contain enough moisture, lenticular clouds can form as the water vapor rises and cools into water droplets. Drier waves of air do not produce clouds.

Moist air

Dry air

Moist air

Dry air

Mountain

Wave clouds

Kelvin-Helmholtz clouds are amazing clouds that look like waves breaking on a beach. They form when a stream of air flows over a layer of cloud, carving wavy shapes into the top.

The clouds stay perfectly still and appear to hover.

Lenticular cloud

These beautiful clouds look like floating pancakes or saucers.

Over the past century, there have been many claimed sightings of mysterious alien spacecraft low down in the sky. None have proved to be real, so what exactly did people see? We may never know for sure, but it's likely some observers were looking at unusual clouds! Clouds can take on lots of curious shapes that may remind us of anything from dinosaurs to ocean waves, hats, and people's faces.

One special cloud formation could easily be mistaken for a spaceship in the distance because it is thin, smooth, and rounded, like a huge white saucer. It is known as lenticular cloud and occurs in mountainous areas, but only in certain conditions. A strong, moist wind has to be blowing directly across the mountains to create waves of rapidly moving air full of water vapor. We can't see the waves, of course, although we can see the clouds that are produced above the peaks and on the downwind side of the mountains. Aircraft steer clear of clouds like these, because they're a sign of powerful air currents.

Each dollop of lenticular cloud is roughly disk-shaped, with smooth edges.

Lenticular cloud

Most lenticular clouds are spotted in winter, when winds are strongest. Sometimes groups of them pile up over mountain summits like stacks of pancakes.

Clouds of water

The puffy white or gray formations we call clouds form when water vapor, which is a gas, condenses into water droplets or freezes into ice crystals. Each cloud contains billions of tiny droplets or crystals.

The clouds line up with the mountain ridge.

163

Green glow

Strange lights flicker through the night sky during the winter at the poles of the Earth. Known as the northern or southern lights, they are usually green—but can also be yellow or red—and swirl around like smoke. They occur when tiny particles from the sun hit gases in the Earth's atmosphere and release their energy.

CHAPTER 4

Earth

Our planet has many extraordinary features on land, at sea, and deep underground, many of which took millions of years to form. Among them are bright pink beaches, glittering golden fossils, and caves packed with giant crystals. Some of these features look like they could have been made by people, but they are all natural. A few can even tell us about the very beginnings of life on Earth.

Stromatolites grow just 0.02 in (0.5 mm) a year.

Lots of layers

Stromatolite fossils have complex folds and wavy bands that show the layers of material from which they were made.

This stromatolite fossil looks and feels similar to rock.

The layers of the stromatolite are still visible within the fossil.

Stromatolites today

Most stromatolites alive today are found on the coast of Western Australia, such as these in Shark Bay. They can be seen in shallow water, where there is lots of sunlight.

Stromatolite

These rocky formations are some of the earliest evidence of life on Earth.

For most of our planet's history, the only signs of life were strange mounds scattered in shallow water. Some of them were as large as basketballs, others much smaller. These were stromatolites. They looked like regular rocks but were actually made by life-forms, called cyanobacteria, or blue-green algae. The bacteria grew into colonies and oozed out a kind of glue, which stuck specks of sand and mud together. Over time, this created mushroom-shaped rocks. Sunlight gave the bacteria their energy, and as they harvested it, they released oxygen. This boosted the planet's oxygen levels, meaning many other living things were later able to develop, including plants, animals, and eventually humans. So, without stromatolites, you might not exist!

The most ancient stromatolites appeared 3.5 billion years ago. However, the bacteria inside them are long since dead and they have transformed into fossils. You can still see living stromatolites in a few parts of the world, although these are much younger—just a few thousand years old. They occur in shallow salt water along the coast and in inland lakes.

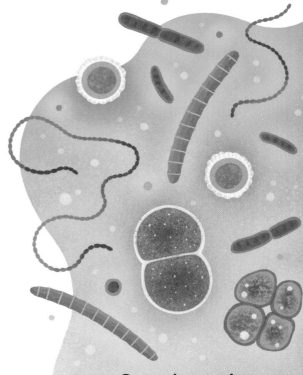

Cyanobacteria

The tiny organisms that make stromatolites are called cyanobacteria. There are many different types, but they all live near the water's surface and perform photosynthesis.

How a stromatolite forms

1. Sand and mud settle on a shallow seabed and cyanobacteria grow on top in a slimy mat.

2. Particles of sand and sediment get trapped by the mat and are glued together into a layer of rock.

3. Over a long stretch of time, layers of rock and dead bacteria build up to create a solid mound.

Petrified Forest

Dead tree trunks can turn into fossils over time, and when this happens, we say the wood is "petrified." The Petrified Forest in Arizona has large numbers of colorful chunks of these fossilized trunks.

The hexagonal pillars are made of basalt, a hard volcanic rock.

Minerals such as quartz have replaced the woody material.

Giant's Causeway

Volcanic eruptions long ago created this spectacular feature on the coast of Northern Ireland. The jumble of rock pillars was said to have been built by a giant who wanted a walkway across the sea.

Rock formations

All over the world, there are jaw-dropping rock sculptures made by natural forces. They were created by geological activity and carved by the wind, rain, and flowing water. It took millions, sometimes billions, of years to make them, and they are still being shaped to this day.

Valley of the Moon

In northern Argentina, there is a strange rocky landscape like the surface of the moon. The pale rock has been sculpted by the wind into extraordinary shapes and contains many dinosaur fossils.

Richat Structure

Seen from space, this formation is like a colossal eye staring out of Africa's Sahara Desert. It is more than 25 miles (40 km) wide and formed from a dome that has been eroded to reveal the rings of rock inside.

Karlu Karlu boulders

The boulders of Karlu Karlu are a collection of huge granite rocks in the north of Australia. Some are so worn and rounded, they seem to be about to topple over and roll away.

Vermillion Cliffs

There are many stunning landforms in the southwestern US, including the Vermillion Cliffs in Arizona. These swirls of rock, made mostly of sandstone, were formed by ancient flowing water and windblown sand.

White Desert

We often think deserts have lots of yellow sand, but, although some do, many don't. This one in Egypt is famous for its snow-white sandscapes and tall pillars. Many are made of chalk, a kind of limestone.

Zhangye National Park

The sandstone in this part of China is incredibly colorful thanks to the different minerals in the rock. Movement in the Earth, together with the wind, sun, and rain, created the formations we see today.

Chalky shells

Forams build their shells from calcium carbonate, the same material as chalk. They extract the ingredients for it from seawater as they grow.

The sand looks pinkest in the warm glow of sunset.

The holes in the shells are where the foram's tentacles reached out from.

Grains of pink sand are the same size as those of ordinary sand.

Sand formation

Waves and crashing surf slowly grind the sea strawberry shells together and make them smaller, until they eventually become sand.

Star sand

A few forams have star-shaped shells that create a special type of sand, called star sand. There are beautiful star sand beaches on the Okinawa Islands in the south of Japan.

Pink sand

There are astonishing rosy beaches made from billions of tiny shells.

On a few sheltered coasts in the Caribbean, Mediterranean, and by the Pacific Ocean, you can walk across bright pink sand. Entire beaches here are the color of cherry blossom or strawberry-flavored milk! The spectacular sand formed in an unusual way, from the remains of microscopic creatures known as "forams"—short for foraminiferans. Some forams drift near the surface of the ocean, others attach to the ocean floor, but all of them construct amazing shell-like skeletons to live in. When they die, their shells gather in a thick layer on the seabed and then, over a long period of time, they are swept ashore to create sandy beaches. Only some forams have pink shells, which is why pink sand beaches are so rare.

When forams build their shells, they absorb traces of chemicals in the ocean. This means scientists can examine the fossils of ancient forams to learn about the chemistry of the ocean long ago. They are even able to figure out the temperature of ancient oceans to show how the Earth's climate has changed over vast periods of time.

Pink Sands Beach

One of the most famous pink beaches is in The Bahamas, a country in the Caribbean. Pink Sands Beach attracts tourists from all over the world.

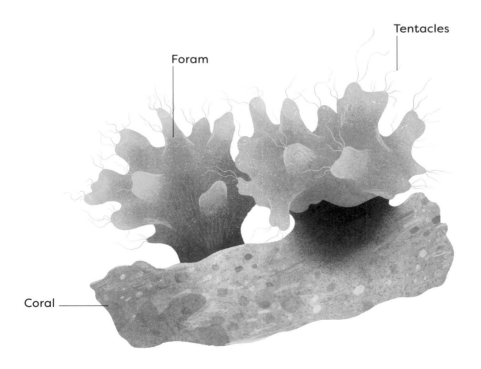

Tentacles

Foram

Coral

Pink forams

These types of foram have rosy colored shells. They attach themselves to coral in tropical seas and push tentacles through holes in their shells to catch minuscule mouthfuls of food, such as algae and bacteria. When they die, their leftover shells retain their pink color.

Golden fossil

Some fossils appear dazzling, as if made from precious metal.

There are extraordinary fossils with a stunning golden appearance that look almost too good to be true. Most fossils are a dull color—either gray, brown, or black, much like the rock in which they formed. These, however, seem to be made of gold! In fact, the glittering, yellow substance is a mineral called pyrite. People sometimes call it "fool's gold," because gold miners used to mistake it for the real thing.

For golden fossils to occur, conditions have to be just right. They develop in deep seas with large amounts of iron and sulfur. When a sea creature dies here and drifts to the bottom, something strange happens. Once its soft parts have rotted away, bacteria cause the sulfur to react with the iron to produce pyrite, and this is what replaces the hard parts of the sea creature. Most pyrite fossils are made from the shells of ancient sea animals such as spiral-shelled ammonites or squidlike belemnites, but golden fossils of dinosaur bones, shark teeth, and plants also exist. These fossils must be stored carefully when discovered, though—if kept in humid air, they will eventually turn to dust.

Pyrite

Pyrite is a mineral made from iron and sulfur. It can grow in a variety of amazing shapes, including cubic crystals that you might think were created on a computer.

How a fossil forms

1. A belemnite dies and its body sinks to the seabed. The soft parts of its body rot away, leaving only its hard internal shell.

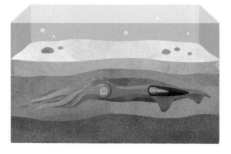

2. The shell is buried by mud, sand, and other sediment. Over time, the sediment slowly turns to rock under the pressure from above.

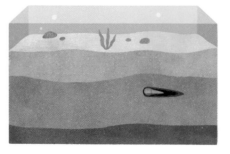

3. Slowly, the hard shell is replaced by minerals. After millions of years, this produces a perfect copy of the shell, made from rock—or pyrite.

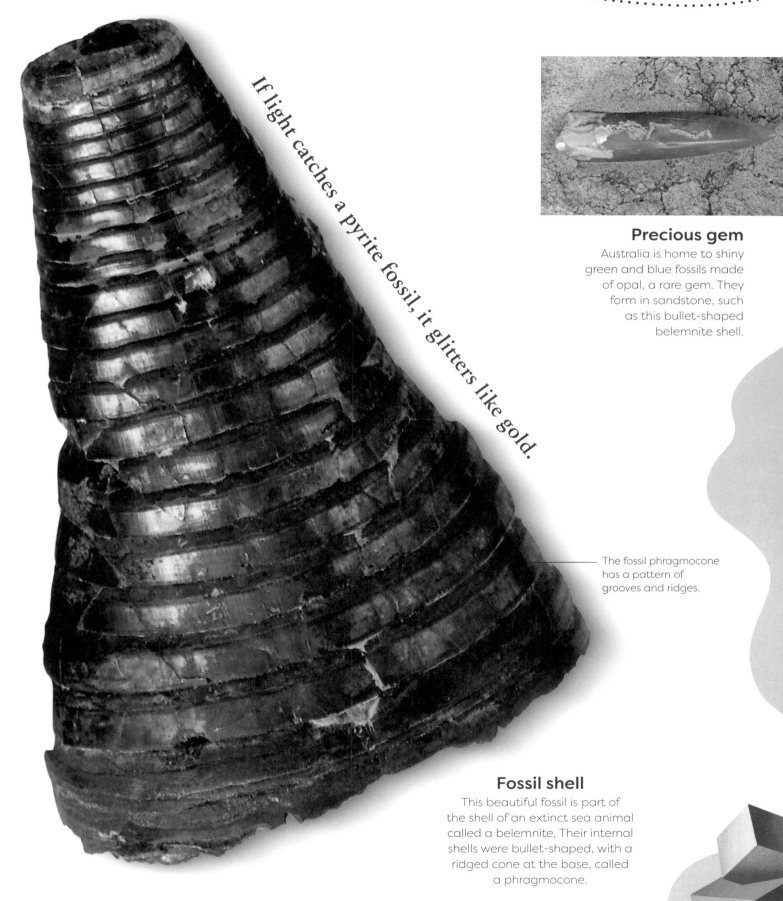

If light catches a pyrite fossil, it glitters like gold.

Precious gem
Australia is home to shiny green and blue fossils made of opal, a rare gem. They form in sandstone, such as this bullet-shaped belemnite shell.

The fossil phragmocone has a pattern of grooves and ridges.

Fossil shell
This beautiful fossil is part of the shell of an extinct sea animal called a belemnite. Their internal shells were bullet-shaped, with a ridged cone at the base, called a phragmocone.

175

Cat's eye shine

When moonstone is cut and polished to make it round, the curved surface may glint with a single line of light, like the narrow pupil in a cat's eye. It is now called cat's eye moonstone. This type of light reflection is known as chatoyancy.

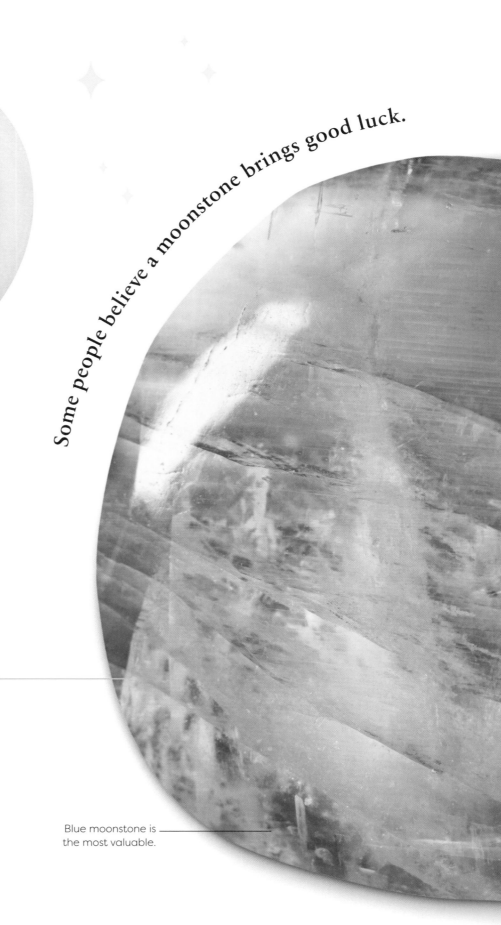

Some people believe a moonstone brings good luck.

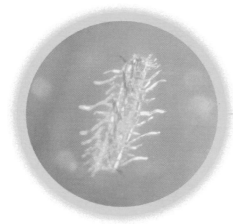

Tiny cracks

If you examine moonstone under a microscope, you will often see tiny cracks. They are called "centipedes," after the many-legged creepy-crawlies.

Blue moonstone is the most valuable.

Moonstone

Like moonlight, this gorgeous stone has a magical shine.

When the moon is full, its glowing reflection seems to dance on the surface of water. Shimmering moonlight is one of the most spellbinding sights in nature. There are unusual stones that produce the same kind of effect, and we call them moonstones. If you turn them in your hand, they twinkle and shine, which is caused by light reflecting off small pieces of mineral in the stone. They may be different colors, but the most beautiful are milky white or pale blue, and so clear you can almost see through them. The raw stones are rough and uneven at first. However, skilled jewelers are able to cut and polish the stones to transform them into gems, which are used in rings, brooches, and precious ornaments.

Moonstones have been found on most continents, although many of the finest blue examples come from Sri Lanka and other parts of southern Asia. Numerous legends have grown up around these special stones. Pliny the Elder, an ancient Roman writer, thought they changed appearance to match the phases of the moon.

Polished moonstone has a delicate surface that shimmers as you turn it.

Moonstone

Several varieties of mineral are known as moonstone. They contain a mixture of elements, including sodium, potassium, aluminum, silicon, and oxygen.

Rocks and minerals

Earth's rocks, and the minerals from which they are made, come in a mind-blowing variety of forms. Some also have unexpected qualities—for example, they may be very soft, magnetic, bendable, or catch the light in strange ways.

Blue amber

Amber is an unusual kind of mineral-like fossil that develops slowly from the hardened resin of conifer trees. Usually, it is golden, like honey, but rare varieties reveal a blue color in sunlight.

Sideromelane

When underwater volcanoes erupt, the red-hot lava reacts with seawater to create intriguing rocks. They include sideromelane, which is yellowish and made from a network of volcanic glass.

Phantom quartz

Quartz is a common mineral but there are many types. One of the most mysterious is phantom quartz, which gets its name from the ghostly outlines of the layers of crystals you can see within it.

Watermelon tourmaline

Tourmaline is a group of minerals that come in a wide range of colors, and this variety is so bright you might not believe it's natural. Its crystals are pink and green, just like a slice of watermelon!

Soapstone

Not all rocks are hard. Soapstone, for example, is so soft it can be scratched with a fingernail. It feels flaky or greasy, and contains lots of talc, one of the world's softest minerals.

Chalcanthite

Chalcanthite contains a form of copper that gives it a dazzling blue or blue-green color. It often hangs from the ceiling of caves and mines as spectacular spikes called stalactites.

Septarian nodule

The strange patterns in this nodule, or lump of mineral-filled rock, seem to have been made by an artist. In fact, they formed over millions of years as different minerals filled the cracks in a piece of mudstone.

Cracks in the nodule contain minerals of different colors.

Grape agate is usually a shade of purple.

Grape agate

This peculiar type of mineral is actually made from chalcedony, not agate. It looks like a bunch of grapes, which is a shape known as botryoidal (pronounced "bot-ree-oi-dull"). It is very rare and found mainly in Indonesia.

Colossal crystals

Deep beneath a mountain in Mexico lies the Cave of the Crystals. Giant white crystals grow out of its walls, floor, and roof like frozen laser beams. Some are longer than a bus! They are made of the mineral gypsum and formed millions of years ago when hot volcanic water poured into the chamber.

Life at the limit

Living things that can survive in extreme habitats are called extremophiles. Flamingos are an example—they often wade in hot salt lakes full of chemicals that would burn our skin.

Cloudy black fluid belches from the vent chimneys.

The "smoke" contains toxic chemicals, such as hydrogen sulfide, and is as acidic as lemon juice.

Fluid from the vent cools fast and its minerals turn solid. They are added to the vent chimney, which grows up to 12 in (30 cm) a day.

Outer space

Europa, a moon of the planet Jupiter, has a deep, ice-covered ocean that might have hydrothermal vents at the bottom. If so, they could perhaps be home to alien life-forms.

Hydrothermal vent

Deep in the ocean, there are rock "chimneys" with a bizarre community of animals.

Scientists used to think the bottom of the deepest oceans was like a desert. Nothing could survive down there, surely? The total darkness, freezing cold, and colossal pressure of the water above would make life impossible. Then, in 1977, a deep-sea submarine made a stunning discovery in the eastern Pacific Ocean. Its crew was amazed to see pillars of rock with strange clouds pouring out, like smoking chimneys. The explorers had found hydrothermal vents. Further missions revealed more about the ultra-tough creatures that swarm all over them. They include giant worms 10 ft (3 m) long, pink fish the shape of tadpoles, white clams the size of dinner plates, and lobsterlike animals with furry claws, called yeti crabs. There are even snails with shiny black shells made of iron!

Hydrothermal vents are the only place on Earth where life is powered not by the sun but by chemicals. Bacteria and other tiny organisms "feed" on chemicals gushing from the vents. They in turn are food for the wonderful animals found here. The first vents formed when the planet was still young—and they may even be where life began.

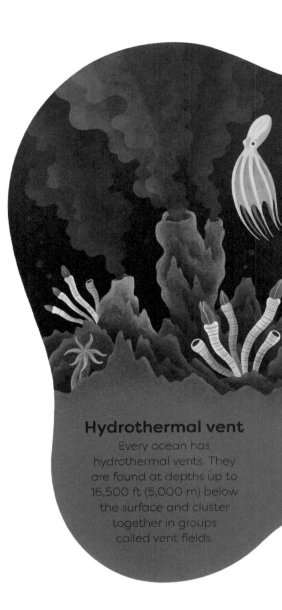

Hydrothermal vent
Every ocean has hydrothermal vents. They are found at depths up to 16,500 ft (5,000 m) below the surface and cluster together in groups called vent fields.

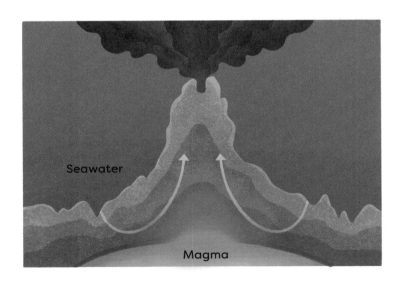

Seawater

Magma

Superheated water
Hydrothermal vents form over cracks in the ocean floor, where the plates that make up Earth's crust pull apart. Ocean water seeps into the deep cracks, where it is heated to as much as 750°F (400°C) and fills with minerals. The superheated water then rises back up and deposits the minerals, creating a vent like a volcano.

183

Weird, but true!

Our planet is naturally weird. In just the last few decades, scientists have been amazed to discover, among many other bizarre things, that plants can scream, fish "talk" through their rear ends, and bees wear perfume to attract mates. Who knows what weird and surprising discoveries we might make next?

Screaming tomatoes

In 2023, Israeli scientists found that tomato plants "wail" when thirsty or their stems are cut. The noise is like bubble packaging popping, but it is too high-pitched for us to hear.

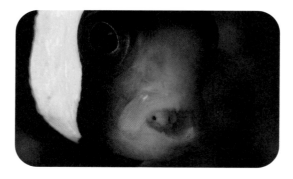

Tongue-eating louse

This sneaky little crustacean grips the tongue of a fish and eats it. Now the poor fish has to use the mouth parasite—still alive—as a freaky replacement tongue.

Scary mouth

On the beaks of baby Gouldian finches, there are four lumps that seem to glow. The strange bumps show the parents where to deliver food in the dark nest.

Poop on the menu

Eating poop is surprisingly common among animals. Baby giant pandas eat their mother's poop to gain the gut bacteria needed to digest tough bamboo.

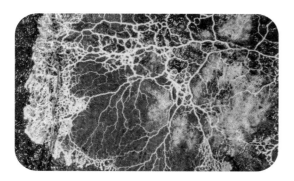

Slime swarm

Slime molds have features of both fungi and animals—and some can move. Their cells join together in a gloopy mass and the slimy threads creep around in search of food.

Farting fish

In 2003, Swedish research revealed that herrings send messages by squeezing air out of their bottoms! The gassy noises enable them to communicate in the dark.

Singing sand

Certain sand dunes appear to sing—but only if their grains of sand are the right size. The mysterious whistling or booming happens when sand is shifted by the wind.

Bee perfume

Male orchid bees collect scent from a variety of flowers, then mix it to create their own fragrance. But why? In 2023, scientists proved that it was to attract female bees.

Glowing minerals

Some minerals, including fluorite and calcite, glow when ultraviolet light is shone on them. They will even glow for a while after the light is switched off.

Lightning sprites

Lightning has several rare and magical forms. Sprites are massive releases of red lightning that shoot high up into the sky, far above the thunder clouds below.

Glossary

alga organism that mostly lives in water and makes food using the energy from sunlight by photosynthesis. Seaweeds are algae

amphibian animal with thin, often slimy skin that can live in water and on land. Frogs, toads, and newts are examples of amphibians

anther top part of a flower's stamen that produces pollen

bacteria microscopic organisms consisting of a single cell each

barbel thin tentacles found on the jaws of some types of fish, used for sensing

bioluminescence release of light caused by a chemical reaction within a living organism

bird animal with feathers and a beak that reproduces by laying hard-shelled eggs. Owls, eagles, ducks, and parrots are all examples of birds

calcium carbonate substance made from calcium, carbon, and oxygen that makes up the rock chalk. It is also found in bones and shells

camouflage appearance of an organism that helps it hide in its surroundings

carbon dioxide substance that is made up of carbon and twice the amount of oxygen. It is a gas at room temperature

cartilage tough, flexible material found inside animals

cell smallest unit of an organism's body that makes up its different parts

chlorophyll green substance in plant cells that absorbs energy from sunlight and allows the cells to carry out photosynthesis

chromosome structure inside a cell that contains genes made from DNA

colony big group of animals that often live in the same home, such as bees in a hive

compound eye type of eye found in invertebrates that is made from many smaller units, each with its own lens

coral group of invertebrates, some of which make hard skeletons that form coral reefs

crustacean type of invertebrate with antennae, many legs, and a tough exoskeleton. Crabs, shrimp, and lobsters are examples of crustaceans

crystal type of mineral form that usually has a geometric shape with many flat sides and straight edges

DNA substance found in all living things that contains the instructions for building its cells

egg cell from which a baby animal grows. On the outside, eggs can be soft, as in amphibians; leathery, as in reptiles; or hard, as in birds

element simplest form of a chemical that can't be broken down further

embryo young organism at an early stage of development found inside a seed, an egg, or a uterus

enamel hard material covering teeth

endangered when a species is rare and might become extinct

equator imaginary line that runs around the middle of the Earth

exoskeleton hard covering that supports the body of some creatures. Exoskeletons must be molted for the animal to grow bigger

fertilization when a male and female cell join together to create an embryo. In plants, male pollen joins with female ovules, and in animals, male sperm joins with female eggs

fish animal with fins and scales that lives underwater. Salmon, eels, and sharks are examples of fish

fossil rock that is the preserved remains or contains the traces of an organism that lived many years ago

fruiting cap part of a fungus that produces its spores. Mushrooms are examples of the fruiting caps of fungi

fungus organism that usually grows in soil and gets its food by digesting the remains of plants and animals. Mushrooms, toadstools, and molds are parts of fungi

gemstone mineral that is colorful or rare and used in jewelry

gene section of a chromosome that determines a particular characteristic of an organism. Genes are inherited and made up of DNA

gill feathery organ that some animals use to breathe underwater

gland organ that makes a particular substance, such as venom or saliva

habitat place where an organism lives—for example, an ocean, rain forest, or desert. Certain life-forms can only survive in specific habitats

hibernation deep sleep that some animals enter during the winter

host organism that another type of organism benefits from. For example, dogs are hosts of fleas, which suck their blood, and other birds are the hosts of cuckoos, which lay their eggs in the host's nest

invertebrate animal with no backbone. Some invertebrates have other internal or external skeletons that support their bodies. Worms, insects, and mollusks are examples of invertebrates

keratin tough material found in some animals. Keratin makes up hair, nails, claws, feathers, and horns

larva young of certain animals, including insects and amphibians. Larvae can look very different from the adult creature

lateral line row of sensors found on the sides of fish, used to detect changes in pressure and movement

magnetic field invisible zone around a magnetic object in which it can attract or repel another object

mammal animal with hair that usually gives birth to its young. Deer, elephants, whales, camels, and rodents are all examples of mammals

melanin dark pigment produced by animals, found in eyes, hair, and skin

metamorphosis process by which certain animals, including insects and amphibians, transform from a larva into an adult

migration process by which certain animals travel a long distance from one place to another, usually to breed or find food

mineral substance made from a specific mixture of elements. Minerals always have crystals and can be brightly colored

nectar sweet liquid made by plants to attract pollinators

neoteny when an animal keeps the features it had when it was young. Fully grown axolotls display neoteny, for example, as they keep their gills from when they were larvae

nest structure built by an animal in which to raise its young

nocturnal description of animals that are awake at night

oxygen element that is a gas at room temperature. Most living things require oxygen to survive

parasite organism that benefits from another organism. Many parasites live on or inside a host's body or in its home and steal its nutrients

photosynthesis process by which plants make sugar using the energy from sunlight

pigment colorful substance. For example, the pigment chlorophyll makes leaves green

poisonous description of an organism that makes poison. Poisons are toxic substances that will kill or damage an organism that eats or touches them

polar description of the areas around the poles, at Earth's northernmost or southernmost points

pollen minute grains produced by male flowers or cones in order for the plant to reproduce

polyp body form taken by some jellyfish and their relatives. Polyps attach to the seabed and have tentacles for catching food. Individual coral animals are examples of polyps

predator animal that hunts and kills other animals, called prey, for food

prey animal that is hunted and killed by other animals, called predators

primate group of mammals that have a large brain. Monkeys, apes, and humans are all examples of primates

protein type of substance made by living organisms. For example, muscles are mainly made of proteins

pupa life stage of an insect when it is going through metamorphosis and it has a hard case with no legs, eyes, or antennae. A caterpillar's chrysalis is a type of pupa

reptile animal with scales that breathes air. Snakes, lizards, crocodiles, and turtles are examples of reptiles

rock substance made from a mixture of minerals. Rocks are usually hard, and they make up the Earth's outer layer

scale small, tough plate that protects the body of some animals. Reptiles and fish are completely covered in scales

sediment tiny piece of a rock or mineral

seed pod case that protects a plant's seeds

silk stretchy substance produced by some invertebrates, including spiders and caterpillars and used to build protective cocoons or webs for trapping prey

species type of organism. Members of the same species can breed together and usually look similar

spinal cord thick bundle of nerves found inside the backbone that carries messages between the brain and body

spore dustlike grains similar to seeds that mosses, ferns, and fungi use to reproduce

stamen male part of a flower that includes an anther, which produces pollen, and a filament

stigma female part of a flower that receives pollen

tentacle long limb of certain animals used to grab food. Corals, octopuses, and squid have tentacles

toxin poison or venom

ultraviolet (UV) light form of light given off by the sun and certain light bulbs that is invisible to humans but that can make some objects and organisms glow

vein tube that carries fluid around plants and animals

venomous description of an organism that makes venom. Venoms are toxic substances that will kill or damage an organism injected with them

vertebrate animal that has a backbone as part of its internal skeleton. Fish, amphibians, reptiles, birds, and mammals are examples of vertebrates

Index

Author Ben Hoare
Illustrator Kaley McKean

Project Editor Olivia Stanford
Designer Sonny Flynn
Project Art Editor Bettina Myklebust Støvne
US Editor Margaret Parrish
US Senior Editor Shannon Beatty
Jacket Coordinator Magda Pszuk
Production Editor Dragana Puvacic
Senior Production Controller Ben Radley
Senior Picture Researcher Sakshi Saluja
Picture Research Administrator Vagisha Pushp
DTP Designer Nityanand Kumar
Managing Editor Jonathan Melmoth
Managing Art Editor Diane Peyton Jones
Deputy Art Director Mabel Chan
Publishing Director Sarah Larter

Consultant Dr. Chris Gibson

First American Edition, 2023
Published in the United States by DK Publishing
1745 Broadway, 20th Floor, New York, NY 10019

Text copyright © Ben Hoare 2023
Copyright © 2023 Dorling Kindersley Limited
DK, a Division of Penguin Random House LLC
23 24 25 26 27 10 9 8 7 6 5 4 3 2 1
001–336584–Oct/2023

All rights reserved.
Without limiting the rights under the copyright reserved above, no part of this publication may be reproduced, stored in or introduced into a retrieval system, or transmitted, in any form, or by any means (electronic, mechanical, photocopying, recording, or otherwise), without the prior written permission of the copyright owner.
Published in Great Britain by Dorling Kindersley Limited

A catalog record for this book is available from the Library of Congress.
ISBN 978-0-7440-8511-2

DK books are available at special discounts when purchased in bulk for sales promotions, premiums, fund-raising, or educational use.
For details, contact: DK Publishing Special Markets, 1745 Broadway, 20th Floor, New York, NY 10019
SpecialSales@dk.com

Printed and bound in China

For the curious
www.dk.com

MIX
Paper | Supporting responsible forestry
FSC www.fsc.org FSC™ C018179

This book was made with Forest Stewardship Council™ certified paper – one small step in DK's commitment to a sustainable future.
For more information go to www.dk.com/our-green-pledge

DK would like to thank: Abi Maxwell for editorial assistance; Laura Barwick for picture research; Neeraj Bhatia and Jagtar Singh for high-res coordination; Caroline Hunt for proofreading; and Susie Rae for the index.

Picture Credits
The publisher would like to thank the following for their kind permission to reproduce their photographs:
(Key: a-above; b-below/bottom; c-center; f-far; l-left; r-right; t-top)

6 Alamy Stock Photo: Minden Pictures / NiS / Oliver Lucanus (cra); Minden Pictures / Flip Nicklin (clb); vkilikov (crb). **7 Alamy Stock Photo:** Creative Nature Media (clb); GL Archive (ca); Tom Stack (cra); Fine Art Images / Heritage Images (cb); Granger Historical Picture Archive, NYC (bc); Kumar Sriskandan (br). **10-11 Alamy Stock Photo:** Minden Pictures / Mark Moffett (b). **11 Shutterstock.com:** Gerry Bishop (cr). **13 Alamy Stock Photo:** blickwinkel / H. Bellmann / F. Hecker. **Shutterstock.com:** Digoarpi (tl). **14 Alamy Stock Photo:** blickwinkel / S. Derder (bl); Risto Hunt (r). **15 Alamy Stock Photo:** imageBROKER / Guenter Fischer (crb); Minden Pictures / Piotr Naskrecki (cla); Henri Koskinen (ca); Chris Mellor (clb); Natural History Library (cb). **Dreamstime.com:** Empire331 (cra). **16 Alamy Stock Photo:** Kike Calvo (clb); Minden Pictures / Thomas Marent. **18-19 Getty Images / iStock:** AlexmarPhoto. **19 Getty Images / iStock:** PeskyMonkey (tr). **20-21 Dreamstime.com:** Dmitry Rukhlenko. **23 Alamy Stock Photo:** All Canada Photos / Julie DeRoche. **Science Photo Library:** Gail Jankus (clb). **24 Alamy Stock Photo:** Scott Camazine (l); KrystynaSzulecka (r). **25 Alamy Stock Photo:** Nature Picture Library / Chris Mattison (crb); Khamp Sykhammountry (cla); Dave Stamboulis (ca); James Peake (cra); Prisma by Dukas Presseagentur GmbH / Kunz Rolf E. (clb); Steve Taylor ARPS (cb). **26-27 Dreamstime.com:** Joloei. **28-29 Alamy Stock Photo:** mauritius images GmbH / Reinhard Dirscherl. **29 Science Photo Library:** Georgette Douwma (br). **30 Alamy Stock Photo:** Nature Photographers Ltd / Paul R. Sterry (br); SeaTops. **32-33 Alamy Stock Photo:** Blue Planet Archive SKO. **33 Alamy Stock Photo:** Sabena Jane Blackbird (tr). **34 naturepl.com:** Juergen Freund (tr). **34-35 Minden Pictures:** Noriaki Yamamoto (b). **36-37 Science Photo Library:** Alexander Semenov. **38 Alamy Stock Photo:** Marcel Strelow (clb). **38-39 Alamy Stock Photo:** Julian Money-Kyrle. **40 Alamy Stock Photo:** Biosphoto / Stuart Wilson (cb); WaterFrame_fur (cl); Lee Rentz (cr). **BluePlanetArchive.com:** Espen Rekdal (clb). **Science Photo Library:** Ted Kinsman (crb); Alexander Semenov (c). **41 Alamy Stock Photo:** David Chapman (b). **Science Photo Library:** Natural History Museum, London (t). **42-43 Alamy Stock Photo:** Eric Nathan. **45 Alamy Stock Photo:** Luc Pouliot. **Getty Images:** Stone / Paul Starosta (tr). **46 Alamy Stock Photo:** Images & Stories (br); WaterFrame_fur (clb). **Dorling Kindersley:** Cotswold Wildlife Park / Gary Ombler (tr, tl). **47 Alamy Stock Photo:** imageBROKER / Guenter Fischer (cb); Minden Pictures / Norbert Wu (cra). **naturepl.com:** Edwin Giesbers (clb); Etienne Littlefair (cla); Chien Lee (crb). **Shutterstock.com:** yamaoyaji (ca). **48 Alamy Stock Photo:** blickwinkel / B. Trapp (tr). **naturepl.com:** Joel Sartore / Photo Ark. **50 Alamy Stock Photo:** Science Photo Library; Science History Images (cla). **52-53 Alamy Stock Photo:** cbimages. **54 Science Photo Library:** Dante Fenolio (cl). **54-55 naturepl.com:** David Shale (b). **56 Alamy Stock Photo:** Adisha Pramod (cra). **naturepl.com:** David Shale (crb); Solvin Zankl (cb). **Science Photo Library:** Nature Picture Library / Doc White (cla); NOAA / Monterey Bay Aquarium Research Institute (clb). **57 Alamy Stock Photo:** Nature Picture Library / David Shale (b); VWPics / Kelvin Aitken (c). **Science Photo Library:** Dante Fenolio (t). **58 Alamy Stock Photo:** Minden Pictures / Richard Herrmann; Minden Pictures / Norbert Wu (br). **61 Alamy Stock Photo:** Nature Picture Library / MYN / Paul van Hoof; Nature Picture Library / Alex Mustard (crb). **62-63 Dreamstime.com:** Verastuchelova. **64 Dreamstime.com:** Hollyharryoz (tr). **64-65 Alamy Stock Photo:** Kike Calvo (b). **66 Alamy Stock Photo:** Minden Pictures / Fred Bavendam (t). **Shutterstock.com:** Eric Isselee (br). **67 Alamy Stock Photo:** Reinhard Dirscherl (cra); David Fleetham (cla); Nature Picture Library / Ingo Arndt (ca); ephotocorp / Rajesh Sanap (clb); Life on white (cb); Itsik Marom (crb). **68 Alamy Stock Photo:** Andrea Izzotti (clb). **68-69 Alamy Stock Photo:** Mark Boulton. **70-71 Alamy Stock Photo:** Minden Pictures / Pete Oxford. **72 Alamy Stock Photo:** imageBROKER / Sohns (clb); Nature Picture Library / Will Burrard-Lucas. **74 Alamy Stock Photo:** Bill Gozansky (b). **Dreamstime.com:** Steve Allen (t). **75 Alamy Stock Photo:** Minden Pictures / Duncan Usher (crb); Nature Photographers Ltd / Paul R. Sterry (clb). **Dreamstime.com:** Hakoar (cla); Isselee (ca). **Getty Images / iStock:** GlobalP (cb); Kerry Hargrove (cra). **76 Alamy Stock Photo:** Avalon.red / Anthony Bannister (clb). **Getty Images / iStock:** GlobalP. **78-79 Guillermo Ferraris and Mariella Superina**. **79 Guillermo Ferraris and Mariella Superina. 80 Getty Images:** Moment / Stan Tekiela Author / Naturalist / Wildlife Photographer (tl). **naturepl.com:** Todd Pusser. **82 Alamy Stock Photo:** Ger Bosma (clb); GFC Collection / animals (cl); Minden Pictures / Cyril Ruoso (c); Mikhail Gnatkovskiy (cr); Aliaksandr Mazurkevich (cb); Diana Rebman (crb). **83 Alamy Stock Photo:** mauritius images GmbH / Plzer Wolfgang (t); J. Dennis Thomas (b). **86 Dreamstime.com:** Martina Unbehauen (clb). **86-87 Dreamstime.com:** Miroslaw Kijewski. **89 Dreamstime.com:** Aaskolnick (cla); Cristina Dini (cra). **Getty Images / iStock:** vainillaychile (bl). **90 Alamy Stock Photo:** Robert Hamilton (br); Nature Picture Library / Alex Mustard. **92-93 Alamy Stock Photo:** Jonathan Plant. **95 Alamy Stock Photo:** Avalon.red / Kevin Schafer (crb). **Shutterstock.com:** Chantelle Bosch. **Wikipedia:** JMK (cr). **96 Alamy Stock Photo:** Albert Wright (tr). **96-97 Alamy Stock Photo:** blickwinkel / B. Trapp (b). **99 Alamy Stock Photo:** Paul Harrison (tl). **Getty Images:** 500px / Martin Anderson. **100 Alamy Stock Photo:** Associated Press / Tosei Kisanuki (cb); imageBROKER / Nigel Dennis (cla); Sari O'Neal (cra); blickwinkel / M. Kuehn (clb); Kseniya Ragozina (crb). **naturepl.com:** Tim Laman (ca). **101 Alamy Stock Photo:** Agami / Brian E. Small (b). **Science Photo Library:** Georgette Douwma (t). **102 Science Photo Library:** Georgette Douwma (clb). **102-103 Alamy Stock Photo:** Marli Wakeling. **104-105 Alamy Stock Photo:** blickwinkel / F. Teigler. **107 Alamy Stock Photo:** Mark Conlin; Reinhard Dirscherl (tr). **108 Alamy Stock Photo:** David Fleetham (br); Nature Picture Library. **110 Alamy Stock Photo:** Biosphoto / Daniel Heuclin; David Fleetham (tl). **112 Alamy Stock Photo:** Design Pics Inc / Carl R. Battreall / Alaska Stock RM; Nature Picture Library / Doug Allan (tr). **114-115 Alamy Stock Photo:** Minden Pictures / Pete Oxford. **115 Alamy Stock Photo:** Christian Htter (cra). **116-117 Alamy Stock Photo:** Minden Pictures / Michael & Patricia Fogden. **119 Science Photo Library:** David M Schleser / Nature's Images (tr). **120 Getty Images:** Stone / Paul Starosta (tr). **naturepl.com:** John Cancalosi. **122 Alamy Stock Photo:** imageBROKER / Bernd Zoller (tc). **122-123 naturepl.com:** Ingo Arndt. **124 Getty Images / iStock:** Andrew Haysom (br). **naturepl.com:** Alex Hyde (t). **125 Alamy Stock Photo:** Brian Hird (Natural World) (cb); Media Drum World (cla); Robert Yone (ca); Ken Griffiths (cra); Donald M. Jones / Minden Pictures (crb). **BluePlanetArchive.com:** Richard Herrmann (clb). **126-127 Minden Pictures:** Takashi Shinkai / Nature Production. **128 Dreamstime.com:** Ecophoto (b). **naturepl.com:** Tui De Roy (tr). **130 Alamy Stock Photo**; WILDLIFE GmbH (br). **132 Getty Images / iStock:** GlobalP (t). **Shutterstock.com:** Andre Coetzer (b). **133 Alamy Stock Photo:** Auscape International Pty Ltd (crb); Malcolm Schuyl (cla); David Fleetham (cra); Imagebroker / Arco / TUNS (clb); Elizabeth Boehm / DanitaDelimont (cb). **Shutterstock.com:** Ryan M. Bolton (ca). **134 Alamy Stock Photo:** Suzi Eszterhas / Minden Pictures (cla); Nature Picture Library / Andy Rouse. **137 naturepl.com:** Nick Garbutt; Anup Shah (bl). **140-141 Alamy Stock Photo:** Larry Doherty. **141 Alamy Stock Photo:** R Kawka (bc). **142-143 Alamy Stock Photo:** robertharding / Lee Frost. **144 Getty Images:** Yoon S. Byun / Portland Press Herald (tr). **Barry A Mills**. **147 Alamy Stock Photo:** Ed Brown Wildlife (tr); Nature Picture Library / Ingo Arndt. **148-149 Dreamstime.com:** Maren Winter. **150 Alamy Stock Photo:** Amar and Isabelle Guillen - Guillen Photo LLC (ca); Nature Picture Library / Georgette Douwma (tr). **BluePlanetArchive.com:** D. R. Schrichte (b). **152-153 Alamy Stock Photo:** Allen Creative / Steve Allen. **153 Getty Images:** DigitalVision / Henrik Sorensen (tl). **154 Alamy Stock Photo:** Amazon-Images (b); Anton Sorokin (t). **155 Alamy Stock Photo:** Guillermo Lopez Barrera (cla); Perky Pets (cra); Matthijs Kuijpers (clb); David Boag (crb). **Dreamstime.com:** Dan Rieck (ca). **naturepl.com:** MYN / Paul van Hoof (cb). **157 Alamy Stock Photo:** Michele Burgess (crb). **naturepl.com:** Joel Sartore / Photo Ark. **158 Alamy Stock Photo:** Jrgen Kottmann. **Wikipedia:** Jerzy Opioa (cla). **160-161 Alamy Stock Photo:** GC Stock. **162 Alamy Stock Photo:** John Davidson Photos (cla). **162-163 Getty Images:** Photodisc / Don Smith (b). **164-165 Alamy Stock Photo:** Nature Picture Library / Jack Dykinga. **168 Alamy Stock Photo:** Jane Gould (bc). **Shutterstock.com:** michal812. **170 Alamy Stock Photo:** Richard Maschmeyer (tr). **Dreamstime.com:** Kevin George (b). **171 Alamy Stock Photo:** All Canada Photos / Karen Crowe (clb); Charlotte Rhodes (cla); katacarix (cra); Stephen Belcher / Minden Pictures (cb); Argentique76 (crb). **NASA:** (ca). **172 Depositphotos Inc:** siimsepp (br). **David Fenwick**. **175 Alamy Stock Photo:** John Cancalosi (tr). **176 Holts Gems:** (clb). **176-177 Shutterstock.com:** vvoe. **178 Alamy Stock Photo:** Natural History Museum, London (clb); WILDLIFE GmbH (cra); Siim Sepp (cb). **Dreamstime.com:** Hguerrio (crb). **Shutterstock.com:** Ansis Klucis (cla). **James St. John:** (ca). **179 Alamy Stock Photo:** Nature Picture Library / John Cancalosi (t). **Shutterstock.com:** Cagla Acikgoz (b). **180-181 Science Photo Library:** Javier Trueba / MSF. **182 Alamy Stock Photo:** GM Photo Images (tr). **Getty Images:** Ralph White (b). **184 Alamy Stock Photo:** Keren Su / China Span (crb); Mike Veitch (cr). **Getty Images / iStock:** lucentius (cl); merve_t (clb). **185 Alamy Stock Photo:** George Grall (cr); Morley Read (tl); Frank Hecker (tr); Mark Taylor / Nature Picture Library (cl); Floris van Breugel / Nature Picture Library (clb); John Sirlin (crb)

Cover images: Front: Alamy Stock Photo: Mark Conlin (clb), Larry Doherty (cl), FLPA (cra), Minden Pictures / Pete Oxford (tl), Nature Picture Library / Alex Mustard (br); **Dreamstime.com:** Isselee (tr); **Barry A Mills:** (bl); **Shutterstock.com:** Luc Pouliot (cr), vvoe (crb); **Back: Alamy Stock Photo:** Minden Pictures / Richard Herrmann (tr), Minden Pictures / Thomas Marent (tl); **Shutterstock.com:** Cagla Acikgoz (br), Ryan M. Bolton (bl)

All other images © Dorling Kindersley